Masterpieces in Steam

Masterpieces in Steam

Written and photographed
by
COLIN D. GARRATT

LONDON
BLANDFORD PRESS

First published 1973

© 1973 Blandford Press Ltd,
167 High Holborn, London WC1V 6PH

ISBN 0 7137 0637 6

All the photographs in this book were taken with a Praktica camera using 50-mm Tessar and Pancolar lenses and a 135-mm Zeiss lens, on Agfacolor C.T. 18 reversal film

Colour section printed in 4-colour lithography
by Colour Reproductions Ltd, Billericay.
Text computer typeset in 9 point Baskerville, printed and
bound by C. Tinling & Co. Ltd, London and Prescot

INTRODUCTION

I often liken the photography of locomotives to portrait photography, for the subject always looks different depending upon the camera viewpoint selected. Of course, most people look better from certain selected angles, but this must always be subjective; likewise with locomotives, for even when the viewpoint selected is a general one, it may not heighten some particular aspect of the subject which an onlooker would have liked emphasising. Add to this the complexity of a locomotive's working environment and immediately we pass to the realms of subjective visual experience, for whilst certain elements such as signals, stations, viaducts and tunnels are intrinsically a part of the railway setting, exactly how the individual sees them in relation to the subject must be personal. I do not make these points as a lament, but simply to establish some basic criteria by which the art-work on the following pages might be judged, if not actually appreciated. Therefore, having banished any possibility of an 'ultimate truth', I have tried to portray the vitality of these locomotives in their working environments and intend, as this series progresses, to come ever closer to this ideal.

It would be an act of gross irresponsibility upon my part to undertake a set of books such as these without careful selection and research on which types of locomotive to include and consequently it will be my intention to give as wide a range of types as possible, but with especial emphasis on the many distinctive families of locomotives the world over. However, good coverage will be given to the more specialised gems which still exist in various parts of the world.

As stated in the first volume, this series is intended to be a combination of Art, History and Adventure. Accordingly I have provided a reasonably voluminous text giving the story and historical details of each type illustrated, along with some of my impressions and

5

adventures when filming them. Painstaking care has been taken to ensure accuracy. Inevitably, authorities differ on certain facts. Nevertheless, the vast amount of information provided has been verified by the organisations to which it relates.

My experiences in making this book were very diverse, ranging from all-night photographic sessions in British collieries, night footplate riding over the Arctic Circle in blizzards and filming the very last steam engines in France, to my many adventures in Yugoslavia with that country's author and photographer Tadej Bratè who, despite never failing to remind me of the malevolence of western life, was a wonderful companion. Already work is in hand for the third and fourth volumes of the series and as my travels become ever more widespread I never fail to be amazed by the widely differing array of countries encountered and their attitudes towards my researches: some co-operative, some hostile, some coldly indifferent and others, like Finland, warmly helpful in every conceivable way.

Work such as this relies upon assistance from many people and therefore I must formally thank the many friends and acquaintances who have so willingly assisted me during the preparation of this volume: Horace Gamble, Dr and Mrs J. Hampton, Mrs M. E. Warner, Allen Civil, Colin E. Mountford, L. G. Charlton, R. T. Russell, W. K. Williams, Ken Plant, Derek Knott, Bill Parkes, George Edlin, Jack Staley, Cyril Tolley, Judith Hampton, Roger West, Eero Tuurna, Mauno Tahvonen, Ilkka Hovi, Hammes Peltola, Tadej Bratè, Marijan Vidmar and Rozka Pajntar and family. My thanks, too, to the following organisations: Hudswell Badger Ltd, Finnish State Railways, Italian State Railways, French National Railways, British Embassy, Belgrade, and Ž.Z.T.P. Ljubljana, and to David Thornhill, along with his monthly publication *World Steam* (available from 124, Wendover Road, Stoke Mandeville, Aylesbury, Bucks.). Lastly, my special thanks, as ever, to Judy Warner.

COLIN GARRATT

November 1972

6

The text refers to a selection of locomotives from the following countries:

Country	Railway company	Gauge
Great Britain	National Coal Board (N.C.B.)	4 ft 8½ in.
	Central Electricity Generating Board (C.E.G.B.)	
	British Sugar Corporation (B.S.C.)	
	British Leyland Motor Corporation (B.L.M.C.)	
Finland	Valtionrautatiet – Finnish State Railways (V.R.)	5 ft 0 in.
France	Societé Nationale des Chemins de fer Francais – French National Railways (S.N.C.F.)	4 ft 8½ in.
Italy	Ferrovie Dello Stato – Italian State Railways (F.S.)	4 ft 8½ in.
	Emilio Astengo Soc., Savona Docks (E.A.)	
Austria	Österreichischen Bundesbahnen – Austrian Federal Railways (Ö.B.B.)	4 ft 8½ in.

From 1921 to 1938, the Austrian Federal Railways took the initials B.B.Ö. Between 1938 and 1945, during the German occupation, they were absorbed into the D.R.B. When they regained their former identity, the initials Ö.B.B. were assumed. Prior to the formation of the Federal Railways separate companies existed, the largest being the K.K.St.B.-Austrian State Railways and the Sudbahn. The splitting up of the Austro-Hungarian Empire in 1918 caused many M.A.V. (Hungarian State Railway) locomotives to pass to other countries.

West Germany	Deutsche Bundesbahn – German Federal Railway (D.B.)	4 ft 8½ in.

After World War II, the railways of Germany were divided and the pre-war title of Deutsche Reichsbahn (D.R.) was taken by the newly-formed East Germany, while West Germany's railways became the D.B. The initials D.R.B. have been used in the text to denote the pre-war German railways and thus differentiate them from the present-day D.R.

Yugoslavia	Jugoslovenske Zeleznke – Yugoslav Railways (J.Z.)	standard 4 ft 8½ in. narrow 760 mm

Upon the formation of Yugoslavia in 1918, the railways were initialled S.H.S. – Kingdom of Serbs, Croats and Slovenes. In 1929 the name 'Kingdom of Yugoslavia' was used and the railways then became J.D.Ž. – Yugoslav State Railways. After World War II this was abbreviated to simply J.Ž. In common with Austria, parts of Yugoslavia came under German rule during World War II, and some engines were taken into D.R.B. stock, whilst certain areas regained their former pre-Yugoslav identity, but where relevant this has been elucidated in the text. After World War II the Yugoslav State Railway was reinstated as before.

BRITISH INDUSTRIAL STEAM LOCOMOTIVES

Unlike many contemporary writers upon railway subjects I place an immense importance on the locomotives in industry and regard them in many respects as being every bit as significant historically as their main line counterparts. For this reason I have included a liberal selection of interesting British industrials some of which are still extant at the time of writing. Documentation of such engines has over the years been poor, notwithstanding the appearance of several excellent books on the subject during the last five years, whilst detailed studies of industrials in other countries are virtually non-existent. Hence it will also be my policy to feature these alongside main line engines as this series develops throughout the world. As late as 1972, five years after the basic extinction of steam in Britain, several hundred industrial locomotives still exist – offering a wealth of interest, charm and splendour. The diverse lineages of these machines may often be traced back as far as the 19th century. Who indeed could mistake a typical Peckett, Andrew Barclay or Hawthorn Leslie? In all, Britain has had over 200 locomotive builders and many offered a range of standard designs which invariably embodied the firm's traditional characteristics.

It is interesting to reflect, one-and-three-quarter centuries later, that the world's first steam locomotive was an industrial in a South Wales colliery and that the production of this engine gave a momentum to the industrial revolution that can still be felt today. After this first locomotive was introduced it was over 20 years before steam engines graduated onto main lines, all early engines being employed in industry, hauling coal to foundries or loading staiths on rivers and canals. Once main line companies became established they constructed their own locomotive works, but a vast future lay ahead for the private builders for, apart from supplying engines to collieries, iron works, docks and construction companies, they were also to serve a vast overseas market, created as a result of Britain's pioneering the railway age. Accordingly Britain supplied steam locomotives for export-over one-and-a-half centuries, during which time British engines went to almost all corners of the globe. Thousands of these engines, both main line and industrial, are still extant, especially in Africa, India and South America, and many will be covered in later volumes. As Crewe, Doncaster and Swindon have become known historically as railway towns, owing to their being the headquarters of large main line companies, so amongst the private builders has Leeds predominated in being the centre for such famous firms as Kitsons, Manning Wardle, Hudswell Clarke and Hunslet, and although it is not generally remembered as a railway town, Leeds has constructed more steam locomotives than any other British city. Not far behind is Newcastle upon Tyne where the brilliant Robert Stephenson established the world's first locomotive works in 1823. Newton-le-Willows in Lancashire is the home of the Vulcan Foundry while north of the border Kilmarnock is known for Andrew Barclay and Glasgow recalls the North British Company, a prolific exporter of main line and industrial engines. A locomotive on a plinth in Stafford bears testimony to Bagnalls, the greatest locomotive producers in the Midlands, while Bristol in the south-west is the home of both Peckett and Avonside engines.

Such a heritage has been somewhat eclipsed by the main line railway for although these trojans of industry were responsible for the movement of much bulk they were often unseen and unheard, overshadowed by cooling towers, slag heaps and blast furnaces despite the fact that with boundless verve they almost blew their insides out hauling loaded trains through industry's mazes. With names to intrigue, many boasted huge brass plates bearing their building date and maker's name and a prominent feature of these engines was their terrific age, many having come from builders long since defunct. The ideal circumstances of one driver, one engine, were often responsible for their immaculate condition, with shiny cab fittings and gleaming exteriors, showing how affectionately the men tended their steeds. Another reason for these engines' being overlooked was that their single track systems seemed to defy recognition; though abounding almost everywhere, they passed unnoticed over tiny road bridges or ungated crossings. If, however, one was lucky enough to locate them and follow the courses of their tracks, the inner complexities of our industrial world were revealed.

Fortunately present-day social enlightenments combined with the necessary economic resources have enabled Britain to save many of these engines from complete annihilation and nowadays preserved railways throughout the country offer considerable evidence of industrial locomotive traditions. Magnificent as this achievement is, it does lack that *pièce de résistance* of the steam engine – its working and industrial environment. Countless thousands of industrial engines have roamed all corners of Britain, yet only such engines as those illustrated now remain. Apart from dieselisation, industrial rationalisation has done much to reduce industrial railway networks, whilst road transport, tractors, caterpillar vehicles and of course the 'Clean Air Act' have all combined to decimate the steam engine.

We, with our present-day colour films, must capture what is left, before extinction comes, some time during the present decade. Although quite a number of engines remain, materials and spares are becoming notoriously difficult to obtain – even, I am told on good authority, for such classes as the Hunslet Austerities – and so often the eventual production of such materials extends beyond the grounds of economic feasibility. Many fine engines have recently gone to breakers' yards for the need of just a new set of tyres.

As the steam age, if not the railway age itself, recedes into history a new set of places comes to the fore to be remembered as the last to retain a working steam complex. The ones featured in this volume are typical, remote and unheard-of places such as Cadley Hill in Derbyshire, Backworth in Northumberland, Waterside in Ayrshire and Polkemmet in West Lothian. In such places as these will die one of Britain's most priceless pieces of industrial history and achievement.

Cadley Hill No. 1 Austerity 0–6–0ST

Plate No. 15

It seems quite out of context for a colliery engine to be in far better external condition than the majority of preserved ones but this is the case with Cadley Hill No. 1, an engine permanently maintained in the sparkling condition shown. This was the last steam engine sent to Cadley Hill Colliery and its resplendent green livery makes a fine contrast with the other two locomotives there, the red R.S.H. 0–6–0ST and the blue W.B. 0–6–0ST – see plates 31 and 29 respectively.

The engine is one of the famous Hunslet Austerities whose history was discussed in *Twilight of Steam,* the first volume of the series. It was actually built at Hunslet's Leeds Works as No. 3851 in 1962 and was one of the last three Austerities built, the final two following in 1964.

11

1 **WINTER IN FINLAND** with a V.R. Tv1 class 2−8−0 struggling out of the Hyrynsalmi Sand Quarries with a loaded train.

2 **ADIEU TO THE 141R.** One of the last surviving S.N.C.F. 141R 2–8–2s pulls heavily away from Narbonne with freight bound for Spain.

3 **INTERACTION.** An afternoon freight leaves Kouvola behind one of the V.R. standard Tr1 class 2—8—2s.

4 **GREEN DRAGON.** A surviving Peckett B3 0–6–0ST brings a train up to the colli

Brynlliw on the anthracite field of South Wales.

5 **ESSAYS IN FORM (1).** A pair of D.B. 044 class 2–10–0s charge the bank out of Bullay with a 3,000-ton coal train bound for Trier.

6 **ESSAYS IN FORM** (2). Silhouette study of a Hungarian-designed J.Z. 17 class 2–6–2T heading a Sežana–Jesenice train over the western aspects near Korpiva.

7 **ESSAYS IN FORM** (3). Another J.Z. 17 class 2–6–2T heads northwards with a Sežana–Nova Gorica train.

8 **ARCTIC SNOWSTORM.** A day's snowfall at Rovaniemi on the Arctic Cir

cessitates the use of a V.R. Tk3 class 2−8−0 for snow clearance duties.

9   **FIREFLY.** The last Y.E. Workhorse 0–6–0ST heads a load

...in over the Clipstone Colliery system, Nottinghamshire.

10 **WAYSIDE FLOWERS.** A Hungarian-designed J.Z. 17 class 2–6–

...eaks through the Slovenian countryside with a Jesenice–Nova Gorica train.

11 **THE CLIMB TO ŠTANJEL (1).** A J.Z. 36 class 2–10–0 (ex-Prussian) storms the gradient from Prvačina to Štanjel.

12 **THE CLIMB TO ŠTANJEL** (2). A J.Z. 28 class 0–10–0 of Austrian design makes the same heavy weather as its Prussian sister.

13 **LIBERATIONS IN BELGRADE.** British-built Vulcan 2–8–0s (J.Z. 38 c the modern backdrop of Belgrade. In the background is a J.Z. standard 05 Pacif

plied to Yugoslavia by U.N.R.R.A. after World War II lie abandoned against

14 **HUNGARIAN SURVIVOR.** With a shriek from its whistle a J

class 2–6–2T rolls out of Novi Sad depot into the afternoon sunshine.

15 **THE UBIQUITOUS AUSTERITY.** A Hunslet-built Austerity 0–6–0ST in repose between duties at Cadley Hill Colliery, dominated to the rear by Drakelow Power Station.

16 **BURSTING THE TUNNEL.** Near Santa Croce an F.S. 740 class 2–8–0 speeds northwards on a passenger train from Venice to Belluno.

17 **ALL OUT FOR THE SUMMIT.** One of the O.B.B.'s magnificent 97 class 0–6–2 rack/adhesion tanks hammers its way up to Präbichl with empties from Vordernberg.

18 **PRIDE OF THE FLEET.** A standard R.S.H. 0–4–0

...forming night duties at Castle Donington Power Station.

19 **VARIATIONS ON FINNISH 2–8–0s (1).** A V.R. Tk3 class 2–8–0 with spark-arresting chimney shunts amongst the winter snows at Rovaniemi.

20 **VARIATIONS ON FINNISH 2-8-0s** (2). Another V.R. Tk3 class, but with a plain chimney for coal burning, adds a coach to a Helsinki bound express at Oulu.

21 **NORTHUMBRIAN GIANT.** No. 16, the sole surviving example of R.S.H.'s heavy

18-in. 0–6–0STs, pulls away from Eccles Colliery on the Backworth system.

22 **AGAINST WINTER'S SKY.** The last surviving R.S.H. 17

0ST takes a loaded train over the Whittle Colliery branch.

23 **THE WATER STOP.** An Austrian-designed

class 0–10–0 pauses for | refreshment at Štanjel.

24 **HOMEWARD BOUND.** An Austrian-designed 4–6–2T running as the J.Z. 18 class heads a passenger train from Maribor to the Austrian border town of Bleiburg.

25 **CLASSICAL LINES.** This R.S.H. 0–4–0ST at Castle Donington represents a type of locomotive styling prevalent in British industry since the turn of the century.

26 **DAWN AT BACKWORTH.** Another classic shape is this Hunslet-designed Austerity 0–6–0ST built by R.S.H., seen at Eccles Colliery.

27 **GÖLSDORF VETERAN.** An ex-Austrian J.Z. 28 class 0–10–0 departs from Štanjel with a freight for Sežana.

28 **AUTUMN MORNING AT GOLDINGTON.** A windy autumn morning finds one of Goldington's distinctive A. Barclay 0–4–0STs reposing against the cooling towers.

29 **POWER EPITOMISED.** W. Bagnall 0–6–0

...ress in fiery mood at Cadley Hill Colliery.

30 **THE LAST OF THE JUMBOS.** The last Finnish Jumbo – V.R. Tv1 class 2–8

...ds a P.W. Special through the snowy woodlands near Kontiomäki.

31 **INDUSTRIAL TREASURES (1).** *Progress,* an inside-cylinder R.S.H. 0–6–0ST, brings a rake of empty wagons up to Cadley Hill Colliery.

32 **INDUSTRIAL TREASURES (2).** An A. Barclay standard 0–6–0T of 1913 vintage at work on the N.C.B. Waterside system in Ayrshire.

33 **END OF THE 'WORKHORSES.'** The last remaining Y.E. Workhorse 0–6–0ST operates its final haul at Clipstone Colliery prior to being withdrawn from service.

34 **'VICTOR' OF BRITISH LEYLAND.** *Victor*, the famous W. Bagnall 0–6–0ST, hauls a trainload of new cars from the production belt at Longbridge Car Plant.

35 **'THOMAS' OF BRITISH SUGAR.** A Hudswell Clarke 0–6–0T, unofficially
named *Thomas*, caught reposing between night duties at Peterborough Sugar Factory.

36 **SPRING THAW.** As winter relaxes its icy grip upon Finland's rive

Tv1 class 2–8–0 ambles towards Kontiomäki with a freight from Hyrynsalmi.

37 **ESSAY IN WARM BROWNS.** No. 31, the last remaining engine

ries of 18-in. R.S.H. 0–6–0Ts, at Whittle Colliery, Northumberland.

38 **25s ON THE KOČEVJE ROAD (1).** A J.Z. 25 class 2–8–0 of Austrian design on an early morning Ljubljana–Kočevje freight, is seen in the woodlands near Ribnica.

39 **25s ON THE KOČEVJE ROAD** (2). Another J.Z. 25 class 2–8–0, this time heading away from Kočevje with a freight for Ljubljana.

40 **ENGINEERS' SPECIAL.** Caught amongst the woods of Kontiomäki is a V.R. Tv1 class 2–8–0 at the head of a plate-layers' train.

41 **IN ARCTIC SNOWS.** A V.R. Tk3 class 2–8–0 at Rovaniemi on the Arctic Circle.

42　**IMPRESSIONS AT A POWER STATION.** A semi-impressionistic ir

n A. Barclay 0–4–0ST in its working environment at Goldington Power Station.

43 **STRANGE COMPANIONS.** A gnarled lineside tre

...ociation with an R.S.H. 0–6–0T on the Whittle Colliery network.

44 **VARIATIONS AT RIVESALTES VIADUCT (1).** An American-built S.N.C.F. 141R 2–8–2 darkens the morning skies at Rivesaltes viaduct as it heads along the Mediterranean coast with freight for Narbonne.

45 **VARIATIONS AT RIVESALTES VIADUCT (2).** An afternoon perishables train races northwards from the Spanish border behind another S.N.C.F. 141R 2–8–2.

46 **NORTH FROM VENICE.** As evening shadows lengthen an F.S. 625 class 2–6–0 leaves Noale-Scorze with a Venice–Bassano passenger train.

47 **THE SHOTTON BARCLAY.** A veteran A. Barclay 0–6–0ST of 1

its working days at the famous Shotton Colliery in County Durham.

48 **UP AT PENNYVENIE MINE.** The Ayrshire hills resound to the bark
Waterside.

arclay standard 16-in. 0–4–0ST as it storms out of Pennyvenie bound for

49 **VARIATIONS ON ITALIAN 2–8–0s (1).** One of Italy's standard freight engines, the F.S. 740 class 2–8–0, races southwards through Cornuda with a Belluno–Treviso freight.

50 **VARIATIONS ON ITALIAN 2-8-0s (2).** An F.S. Crosti-boilered 741 class 2-8-0 takes a passenger train through the Dolomite mountains from Fortezza to San Candido.

51 **INDUSTRIAL CONTRAST AT POLKEMMET** in the form of a vintage A. Bar
Polkemmet Moor.

–0ST of 1900 and a Hunslet Austerity of 1943, seen storming the gradient up to

52 **RIVALS IN DOCKLAND.** A Deutz 0–4–0 diesel makes poor comparison with one of Emilio Astengo's Henschel 0–6–0WTs in Italy's Savona Docks.

53 **A TALE OF TWO ENGINES.** On the scrapline at Sarajevo (Alipašin Most) the remains of a J.Z. 2 ft. 6 in. gauge rack/adhesion 97 class 0–6–4 make macabre contrast with a condemned J.Z. 83 class 0–8–2.

54 **NIGHT SHUNTER.** The last working example of Finland's Helsinki subur
Pieksamaki.

...s is this V.R. Pr1 class 2–8–2T seen on shunting duties in the snowy woods of

55 **ODE TO EVENING.** An evening study of a J.Z. 33 class 2–10–0 (ex-German

ine) ambling through the Slovenian landscape near Korpiva.

56 **THE PICKUP FREIGHT.** An afternoon freight leaves Imeno on

...ler of Slovenia and Croatia behind a J.Z. 53 class 2–8–2T of Austrian design.

57 **HISTORIC ENGINES AT MARIBOR** (1). The silhouette of a J.Z. 25 class 2–8–0 on the bridge at Maribor makes an exciting contrast with the rising sun.

58   **HISTORIC ENGINES AT MARIBOR (2).** A freight leaves Maribor behind one of the J.Z. 18 class 4–6–2Ts.

59   **HISTORIC ENGINES AT MARIBOR (3).** One of Yugoslavia's standard 2–8–2 mixed traffic engines, the 06 class, leaves Maribor with a passenger train for Cakovec.

60 **LIVING HISTORY.** A J.Z. 28 class 0–10–0 at Štanjel. The engine is ex-Aust

re, the track was cast by Krupp in 1887, and the village is of Roman origin.

61 **IMPRESSION WITH BERRIES.** An impressionistic study showing an R.S.H. 0–4–0ST in contrast with lineside berries at Castle Donington.

When built the engine went to Nailstone Colliery in Leicestershire as one of the famous Hunslet Gas Producer System engines. The Gas Producer was a device which incorporated an underfeed stoker. After 1961 quite a number of Austerities were fitted with the system in an attempt to reduce the emission of black smoke, a factor which caused much concern in many quarters during steam's final years. A number of problems were encountered with this system and it was eventually removed and the engine converted back to traditional firing methods. Evidence is still visible in the small patch on the engine smokebox (see plate). This was once a regulated slide opening for admitting air into the smokebox in conjunction with the underfeed system.

Eventually, Nailstone turned to diesel power and after a period of acting as standby engine No. 3851 was transferred in 1971 to Cadley Hill, where a fine future awaited her. First came the removal of her ugly chimney, a relic from the underfeed system, and its replacement with a standard Austerity one. This chimney was taken from an older Austerity which Cadley Hill had scrapped, and the nameplates of this engine, Cadley Hill No. 1, were conferred upon No. 3851 at the same time. Simultaneously, great care was taken in giving the locomotive its superb green livery, and No. 1 became regarded as Cadley Hill's principal engine owing to its power advantage over the other engines.

Early in 1972 Cadley Hill's maintenance engineers began searching for a spare boiler for No. 1 as the management intended the engine to remain in service over many future years. Accordingly it was deemed prudent to obtain a boiler in a time of relative abundance rather than wait until the Austerities had almost disappeared and spares had become desperately short. This search became intensified later that year when it was found that a slight flaw had developed at the point where the tubeplate bends over to join the inner-firebox wrapper plate; it is said that flaws developing at this particular point constitute one of the few weaknesses in the Austerity design. As yet this flaw is not serious but should it become so, a repair would entail the removal of all 181 boiler tubes for the replacement of the tubeplate and it is felt that fitting a new boiler will be more economical in the long term. Welding could not be employed as No. 1's firebox is copper – a metal not responsive to welding techniques. In passing it is interesting to note that an Austerity's 181 tubes are $1\frac{3}{4}$-in. diameter and give a heating surface of 872 sq. ft. Another 88 sq. ft is provided by the firebox and thus a total of 960 sq. ft is attained.

Such steps towards ensuring No. 1's longevity are well founded, for

Cadley Hill is a colliery with a long future ahead. It is situated on the well known South Derbyshire Coalfield and its railhead is via the Swadlincote branch which connects to the Leicester–Burton-on-Trent line. Adjacent to the colliery is Drakelow Power Station and its cooling towers can be seen dominating the skyline on the colour plate.

Coal has been worked at Cadley Hill for over 100 years but by 1950 the reserves were found to be dwindling, as in fact were those of many surrounding collieries. These diminishing reserves caused much concern and precipitated a deep boring programme carried out beyond the previously assumed coalfield limit. Borings were made to a depth of 3,100 ft and resulted in the discovery of 120 million tons of coal over an area of 12 sq. miles. Overjoyed by the location of such treasure, the N.C.B. approved a major reconstruction scheme at Cadley Hill costing some £4m in order that these newly found reserves could be won. Nowadays Cadley Hill has a daily output of 3,000 tons, giving an annual yield of $\frac{3}{4}$ million tons.

Hence the necessity to locate a spare boiler for No. 1, for when this replacement is obtained it will enable the engine to remain in active service almost indefinitely, thus making the engine a likely contender for being the last of the famous Hunslet Austerities to remain in Coal Board service.

'Progress' R.S.H. 16–in. 0–6–0ST   Plate No. 31

Hawthorn Leslie & Co. were widely known for their range of outside-cylinder saddle-tanks, the company building very few inside-cylinder engines for British industry. Those that were built, however, were very attractive machines and the engine illustrated, R.S.H. No. 7298, is a perpetuation of an old Hawthorn Leslie formula by Robert Stephenson and Hawthorn. The engine was built at Newcastle in 1946 – nine years after Hawthorn Leslie's merger with Robert Stephenson & Co. As with so many modern industrial engines the overall shape can be traced back over many years and in this particular case the engine has a pre-World War I shape, its features being similar to a stud of 15-in. saddle tanks built by Hawthorn Leslie over the earlier years of the century. The exception is that the saddle tank on the earlier engines terminated behind the smokebox; the aura is otherwise identical. Other aspects of this family shape, such as the low curved dome, may be traced by comparing this engine with the outside-cylinder 0–6–0ST depicted on the rear endpaper of *Twilight of Steam*.

94

A number of these 16-in. inside-cylinder engines were built during the 1920s, a well-known example being *Frank* H.L. No. 3534 of 1922, an engine which until recently was working, fifty years later, at Fryston Colliery, Yorkshire. *Progress* was delivered new to Leicestershire's Moira Colliery and was named *Christopher*. In its later years under the N.C.B., *Christopher* was transferred to Measham where the engine's name happened to coincide with that of the colliery manager. Perhaps this gave him fears of expressive faces being painted on the engine's smoke-box front, for this intolerable and potentially jestworthy situation was quickly rectified by none other than the manager himself who obtained the *Progress* nameplates from a nineteenth-century Pecket at Rawnsley Colliery, Cannock Chase, and promptly bestowed these in place of the offending ones. Simultaneously he gave the engine a new and sumptuous red livery, and such was his interest in this distinctive locomotive that upon his transfer to Cadley Hill shortly afterwards he arranged for *Progress* to go too.

As the plate shows, the painting of *Progress* has been superbly done, for it was an attempt to recreate the L.M.S. style of red, the correct number of undercoats and rubbing down all being undertaken during the process. It is extremely refreshing to find an operational industrial locomotive in a pre-nationalisation livery in 1972. Today *Progress* is as fine an engine as any extant in British industry and she is a credit to the South Midlands area of the N.C.B.

No one condemns the operation of sole survivors providing the problematic question of spare parts can be cheaply dealt with, and it became obvious that if Cadley Hill were to maintain such a rare engine as *Progress* then some access to spares must be found. After considerable investigation an identical engine was found out of use at Brookhouse Colliery, Beighton, Yorkshire, in the form of H.L. No. 3726 of 1928. Accordingly staff from Cadley Hill made a visit to Yorkshire to cannibalise this engine of essential parts prior to its being broken up and so *Progress* received a range of excellent spares at scrap prices.

The engine's leading dimensions are: 2 cylinders 16 in. × 24 in., boiler pressure 170 lbs per sq. in., driving wheel diameter 4 ft 1 in. and tractive effort at 85 per cent boiler pressure of 18,110 lbs. Coal and water capcities are $1\frac{1}{2}$ tons and 1,100 gallons respectively, whilst the total length over buffers is 27 ft.

The combination of design and livery of *Progress* fit it well to rural surroundings, for one can imagine it being more than an industrial locomotive, working passenger trains along a rustic country branch line – a feeling heightened by the elegance of its relatively large driving wheels. With these factors in mind I have endeavoured to portray the engine in an amenable environment – for on plate 31 *Progress*'s red livery is poignantly portrayed in contrast to the yellow lineside gorse bushes. In this twenty-six-year-old engine I find an exquisite mixture of ancient and modern and although she lacks the gracefully curved bunker of earlier Hawthorn Leslies, *Progress* has the general appearance of engines loved over former years, and it is much to the credit of Cadley Hill's mechanical staff that the engine survives in perfect working condition today.

'Empress' Bagnall 16-in. 0–6–0ST   Plate No. 29

On page 94 I suggested that one day Cadley Hill might possess the last surviving Hunslet Austerity, but already this colliery is host to two sole survivors, one of which is this highly distinctive Bagnall 0–6–0ST named *Empress*. There are many interesting features about this engine: notice the gaunt smokebox, typical of many Bagnalls ever since the nineteenth century, as are the Ross Pop safety valves which can be seen mounted on the dome. Notice also *Empress*'s squared off saddle-tanks which are another Bagnall characteristic (see also plate 34) although some earlier engines of a closely related class were built with the more conventional rounded ones. Another Bagnall hallmark is the outside cylinders for it is said that Bagnalls never built an inside-cylinder 0–6–0 saddle-tank for industrial use. Accordingly it will be seen that *Empress*'s overall styling typifies many Bagnall products and dates back to the early part of the century.

This type was a standard 16-in. Bagnall design which first appeared in 1944, being a direct descendant of an earlier set of 16 × 22-in. saddle-tanks, and eighteen examples were built over the following twenty-one years. They had two cylinders 16 in. × 24 in., a boiler pressure of 180 lbs per sq. in. and small-diameter driving wheels of 3 ft 6½ in., this combination producing a tractive effort of 22,118 lbs at 85 per cent boiler pressure. The engine's total heating surface is 792 sq. ft, grate area 15 sq. ft, and total weight in full working order 43 tons.

The first one was delivered to Birchenwood Coking Plant whilst many were distributed amongst Staffordshire collieries where the appearance of three engines was greatly changed as a result of an N.C.B. decision to fit them with Giesl Ejectors. The class's other main abode was Preston and seven engines went to the Preston Dock

Authority where they became an integral part of the dockland scene for almost a quarter of a century. One of these engines is now preserved on the Lakeside Railway.

Empress, however, was an exception to the class's general distributive pattern in that she was delivered new from Bagnall's Stafford Works to Moira Colliery, Leicestershire, in 1954. Over the years *Empress* was known as N.C.B. No. 6. She worked at Measham Colliery in the 1960s and it was here that the engine acquired its fine blue livery. In 1965 the manager of Measham Colliery, who had always taken a great interest in this engine, was transferred to Cadley Hill Colliery and he ensured that this attractive blue Bagnall followed him, so bringing it under the protection of this Midlands steam stronghold. Accordingly the engine ran under its own steam over B.R. metals to Cadley Hill, where its number was dispensed with and the name *Empress* was bestowed upon it. The official interest taken in this engine is evidenced by the fact that Cadley Hill's manager obtained *Empress*'s nameplates from a withdrawn Avonside 0–4–0ST at Birch Coppice Colliery, Staffordshire. At the time of the engine's transfer to Cadley Hill it had become the last working example of its kind.

It must be stated that aesthetics do not constitute the sum total of Cadley Hill's endeavours, for the mechanical side is well cared for by an enthusiastic fitting staff and after each working week's operation *Empress,* along with the other engines, is thoroughly checked over with particular attention being paid to injectors, lubrication, brakes, safety valves, cylinder drains, sanding apparatus, blower and all springs, in addition to the standard boiler washouts and smokebox cleaning. Further verificiation of the engine's condition was made at the end of 1972 when *Empress* underwent and passed its hydraulic test. Under this arrangement the boiler's strength is tested by pumping in water up to one-and-a-half times that of the working pressure – this being the amount stipulated by the colliery's insurance company. The test is undergone after removal of the boiler casing and lagging, thus making any leaks visible immediately. Should any leaks occur in the boiler, tubeplates or firebox the engine would not be passed. Conducting a hydraulic test with water ensures complete safety because if steam were used up to such pressures on a seriously fatigued boiler the results would, of course, be disastrous. Hydraulic tests are usually conducted every five years.

With such a fine steam fleet one understands why Cadley Hill indulges in the delightful habit of using diesel as standby, for only in times of emergency will the colliery's Sentinel diesel be found in operation, a reversal of the system employed in virtually every other British colliery. Nowadays Cadley Hill is the mecca for steam enthusiasts in the Midlands and its reputation is growing throughout the country, resulting in an ever-increasing influx of visitors, and as long as these theoretically obsolete machines can be maintained to operate efficiently there will be no change in the colliery's policy of retaining steam.

Andrew Barclay 18-in. 0–6–0ST

Plate No. 32

Early in the nineteenth century the upper valley of the River Doon in Ayrshire was a little-known and remote area possessed of much beauty, but it was not long before the industrial revolution's mushrooming activities took note of the area's huge reserves of coal and ironstone, so resulting in the now legendary Dalmellington Iron Works being created in 1845. The blazing furnaces were fed by an ever-developing network of coal and ironstone mining and the company's railways spread out far into the surrounding hills. The wonderful story of this complex has been eloquently told by David Smith in *The Dalmellington Iron Company*. This book – a classic in railway literature – reads like a full-blooded adventure story and is an evocative account of Dalmellington's engines and men. Its pages abound with the unique folklore of the industrial revolution.

Over much of Dalmellington's history 0–4–0 locomotives were used, but an increase in coal traffic from Pennyvenie, a colliery some three-and-a-half miles south-east of the iron works, necessitated something bigger, especially as gradients as steep as 1 in 44 had to be surmounted, and accordingly the company ordered this fine 18-in. 0–6–0T which arrived new from Andrew Barclay of Kilmarnock in the summer of 1913. She was the largest locomotive Dalmellington had ever received and became known as the 'Big Yin', whilst the number 17 was bestowed upon her by the Iron Company. She became popular with her crews and No. 17 undertook a sixty-year-long career on the Pennyvenie run. Despite various administrative changes over the years she still bears the same number today. No surviving British engine has had so long a continuous working life over one route. The engine's early popularity was somewhat marred in 1918 when on a sharp curve she left the road with a heavy rake of waggons and a man was killed. The exact cause of this accident was not established but an outcome of

98

it was the removal of No. 17's flanges from the centre driving wheels. No further trouble has been incurred throughout her working life. Her wheelbase of 11 ft 6 in. enabled the engine to traverse curves of 192 ft radius. From so long a working life many exploits can be recounted but especially noteworthy was the occasion when she took fifty-three wagons, forty-three empty and ten loaded, over a sinuous 1 in 66 bank. Such a load must have been well in excess of 400 tons and the performance is all the more remarkable when one considers the immense amount of friction to be overcome from the buffers and wheel flanges when traversing sharp curves. This class's hauling capacity designated it as capable of handling 265-ton loads over 1 in 50 grades, 443 tons over 1 in 100, and 636 tons over 1 in 200. Such is the wonderful individuality of steam locomotive performances.

In view of No. 17's superiority over the Barclay standard 16-in. 0–4–0STs used hitherto (see plate 48), a further example of her kind was delivered new in 1923. This engine was numbered 22 and whilst it was almost identical in design there were detail differences in both technical specification and appearance. Firstly, at the Dalmellington Iron Co.'s request No. 22's water carrying capacity was increased to 1,185 gallons as compared with No. 17's 900 gallons – and this extra capacity was more than welcome on the long run up to Pennyvenie. Although both engines had a coal capacity of 35 cwt No. 22 had a squared cab and bunker which gave her a harsher outline and compared very unfavourably with No. 17's curved design. On the technical side No. 22 was given a slightly larger grate area and increased heating surface and, of course, a flangeless centre axle. It is small differences in dimensional details such as these which make the accurate documentation of industrial locomotives very difficult indeed.

After the ironworks closed down the company's collieries were kept in operation until they eventually became incorporated into the N.C.B.'s West Ayr Area and under this new regime another engine arrived of the same class as A.B. No. 2335 of 1953. This locomotive, numbered 24, got away to a terrible start by developing a reputation for poor steaming and no matter who drove her or how she was handled the engine was invariably steam-shy. One can imagine the men's disgust when this new 18-in. engine frequently needed to stop for blowing up on trains which the older A.B. 0–4–0s could work with ease. About this time the N.C.B. were experimenting with Giesl Ejectors and out of sheer desperation this 'dead duck of Waterside' became a candidate. Barclay's men came to fit the Ejector in 1965 at a total cost, including manufacturing rights, of £1,000 (the locomotive's cost when new was just over £10,000). The result was catalytic for not only has No. 24 steamed perfectly ever since, and so become the star of the system, but the men claim a full saving of one ton of coal per eight-hour shift combined with a very noticeable reduction in water consumption. If the men's fuel saving claim is correct, and every driver insists that it is, it would only take some three months to cover the Ejector's cost in terms of coal saving alone, even allowing for only one working shift per five-day week and coal at a relatively low resale price!

Number 24, although ostensibly identical with Nos. 17 and 22, is even harder in outline than No. 22 for apart from incorporating the latter's square cab and bunker she also had sloping side tanks and when the Giesl Ejector was additionally fitted she acquired an almost austere character. It is truly remarkable how a few detail changes make such a radical difference to a locomotive's appearance and when one compares this engine with No. 17 it is hard to believe that they are of the same basic design. Memories of No. 24's better lineage remain however in the form of the original chimney which now lies forlornly amongst long grass in the works yard.

These engines are part of a class of eighteen built by Barclays for use in collieries and steel works over a forty-year period. Other examples of the basic type may still be found at Bedlay Colliery, Glasgow, and at Aberfan Colliery in South Wales. The dimensions of No. 17 are: cylinders 18 in. × 24 in., driving wheels 3 ft 9 in. diameter, boiler pressure 160 lbs per sq. in., grate area 16.3 sq. ft and tractive effort at 8 per cent boiler pressure 23,510 lbs. She has a total heating surface of 980 sq. ft, is $28\frac{1}{4}$ ft long over buffers and weighs 45 tons in full working order. Barclays had a tendency slightly to increase the driving wheel diameter, boiler pressure and grate area of later engines in the class, the latter modification being no doubt owing to the tendency of certain engines to be steam-shy.

Engine No. 22 was withdrawn in the late 1960s and I was pleased to find No. 17, which is by far my favourite, working one sunny morning in 1972. At this time the Pennyvenie run was worked by an A.B. 16-in. 0-4-0ST (see plate 48), as No. 17 frequently ran hot on the rough track and had been relegated to working shale trains from the Dunaskin Washery at Waterside up to the tip at Minnivey (plate 32). Mechanically she was in superb condition as only in 1971 did she receive a thorough overhaul in Waterside Works. It is an avowed intention to work this remarkable veteran over a number of years yet to come. In 1972 No. 24 was similarly undergoing heavy overhaul.

Nowadays, the old Dalmellington system is reduced to a fraction of its former self, but even the surviving fragments bear eloquent testimony to this once remarkable network, evoking images in the mind's eye of the days when the valley was lit by iron furnaces and the sounds of mining rang out for many miles around. Eventually the valley will return to its former tranquility and Dalmellington's surrounding hills will look down as if nothing had ever happened, but it will be many generations before the memories completely die away.

Andrew Barclay 16-in. 0-4-0ST   Plate No. 48

With tales of the old Dalmellington Iron Company on my mind I made my way from Dalmellington village along the lonely road to Waterside. It was a perfect morning for although the sun had barely risen it was already flooding the valley with light and the glistening foliage, soaked with a heavy summer dew, echoed the sun's brilliance, causing a thousand twinkling flashes at each step I took. As I approached Waterside No. 21, a standard 16-in. Andrew Barclay 0-4-0ST, was busily preparing to take a rake of empties up to Pennyvenie Colliery, her black smoke making smudges across the pale blue sky. Waterside is the site of the former Dalmellington Iron Works but nowadays it forms the focal point for a three-and-a-half mile colliery line running south-eastwards to Minnivey Pit and Pennyvenie Colliery, the surviving remnants of this once fine system. One eight-hour shift still operates each weekday with three engines in steam – the workings involving bringing loaded coal trains from Minnivey and Pennyvenie down to the washery and B.R. exchange at Waterside, in addition to taking trainloads of shale from the washery up to Minnivey dump. The method of operation is to assign one engine each for Minnivey and Pennyvenie, whilst the third engine operates the shale trains and shunts the exchange sidings.

I was to ride over this historic three-and-a-half mile route with No. 21 and upon mounting her footplate I was made welcome by the friendliest group of enginemen one could ever wish to meet. With No. 21 ejecting shrouds of steam from the safety valves we set off up the valley with the engine propelling its long rake of wagons over the tortuous grades with fine gusto. Upon reaching Minnivey Mine our pressure had dropped to 120 lbs per sq. in. and in view of the formidable climb from there to our destination, we decided to pause for a 'blow up'. Upon stopping No. 21 was given a liberal dose of coal and a full application of the blower and the healthy roar which ensued assured us that we would not have to wait long. As mentioned on page 98 it was usual for the 18-in. 0-6-0Ts to be used on this run as their extra size invariably dispensed with any necessity to 'blow up' en route, whilst the additional axle ensured greater stability compared with the 0-4-0's wild gyrations. During this temporary respite one could not avoid being aware of the valley's beauty. I momentarily left the engine to survey the quiet rolling hills, which by this time were totally enveloped in rich sunshine. The cry of curlews floated from the hillside above us whilst the beautiful song of a woodlark erupted from a lineside fence. Number 21's whistle broke the quietness just a second before the safety valves lifted, and with a full head of steam we set off again. With our engine in full gear and three-quarter-open regulator we barked our way towards Pennyvenie leaving an acrid trail of black smoke which lazily spread out across the valley below. Over the summit we roared until No. 21 was shut off and allowed to roll down into the colliery yard. The plate shows No. 21 – A.B. No. 2284 of 1949 – up at Pennyvenie as she was preparing to return with the loaded train.

A careful scrutiny of plate 48 will reveal a fascinating aspect of operations at Waterside, which is that all engines carry an improvised tender made from a cut-down colliery wagon. This has been a feature at Waterside for many years and these 6-ton capacity tenders enable the engines to work for several days without a necessity to re-coal. If working hard on the Pennyvenie run a 16-in. A.B. 0-4-0ST might consume up to 2 tons of coal per shift but its bunkers, which are situated inside the cab, only hold 14 cwt. Obviously something had to be done. Whilst the nature of operations at Waterside might be something of an exception a 14-cwt coal capacity for a 16-in. engine is remarkably meagre. Nevertheless it was Barclay's standard practice on many standard designs to dispense with a special bunker in favour of carrying the coal on the footplate. One wonders why. Of course the 18-in. 0-6-0Ts do have separate bunkers and these hold 1¾ tons, but even then coaling up would be necessary at least once per shift. The engine sheds at Waterside cannot accommodate these extra tenders and when the locomotives go on shed their tenders have to be uncoupled and left outside. When the locomotives are not working this antiquated line up of tenders looks remarkably comical.

Ever since 1906 the Dalmellington system has used these 6-ft-wheelbase 16-in. 0-4-0STs, and No. 21 was the last to arrive at

Waterside, being delivered in 1951. Barclays built the type over many years with little basic change in design except that the chimneys became shorter whilst the saddle tanks became deeper, and No. 21 carried 1,030 gallons of water whereas her turn of the century forerunners carried only 850 gallons. Dalmellington's crews certainly got some magnificent work from them as prior to the 18-in. engines' being introduced it was not unusual for one of these engines, banked by a 14-in. 0–4–0ST, to lift trains well in excess of 600 tons across the 1 in 44 gradient up to Pennyvenie; some of the crews even maintained that there was no necessity for 18-in. engines to be introduced at all. One might equate these performances with the standard 16-in. specification which claims an ability to lift 120 tons over a 1 in 25 gradient, 227 tons over 1 in 50 and only 545 tons even up a 1 in 200 bank. Admittedly these figures apply to an unassisted engine but on the other hand the comparison can hardly be said to take account of the immense frictional and physical stresses involved in operations up to Pennyvenie.

Andrew Barclay's engines have predominated at Waterside over many years and it is fitting that a stud of them should survive there today in deference to Scotland's long Barclay tradition. The active stock list in 1972 was three 16-in. A.B. 0–4–0STs and two 18-in. A.B. 0–6–0Ts. Of these five engines two were original Dalmellington Iron Company ones, No. 19, an 0–4–0ST dating back to 1918, and of course No. 17 (see plate 32). No 19 still carries her original boiler and is said to be as good as any engine on the system, excepting No. 24, the Giesl-fitted 0–6–0T. Here then, in this remote Scottish valley, linger fragments from a past industrial era, and the men need no encouragement to discuss all they know of Dalmellington's chequered history. These men are proud of their engines, a fact amply borne out by the heavy overhauls still being carried out at Waterside in 1972.

No. 21 has the following dimensions: cylinders 16 in. × 24 in., driving wheels 3 ft 7 in. diameter and boiler pressure 160 lbs per sq. in., these combining to give a tractive effort at 85 per cent boiler pressure of 19,610 lbs. Total heating surface is 728 sq. ft and grate area $12\frac{1}{2}$ sq. ft, whilst the length over buffers is 25 ft and total weight in full working order 35 tons.

Andrew Barclay 14-in. 0–4–0ST   Plate Nos. 28, 42

When travelling southwards along the ex-M.R. main line one can see, on the eastern side, just to the south of Bedford, the gaunt chimneys of Goldington Power Station. These chimneys serve as a landmark to a fascinating little stud of Andrew Barclay saddle tanks. This modern 180,000-kilowatt power station is situated by the north bank of the river Ouse on land possessing good bearing properties thanks to a preponderance of gravel near the surface. Other advantages of the site are the close proximity of B.R.'s Bedford to Cambridge line, giving access for coal, whilst abundant water for cooling purposes is, of course, available from the Ouse. During the station's construction in the early 1950s two 14-in. 0–4–0STs of a standard design were ordered from Andrew Barclay – numbers 2352 and 2354 – and these engines, which were delivered in 1954, were numbered by Goldington ED9 and ED10 respectively. At the same time Andrew Barclay No.

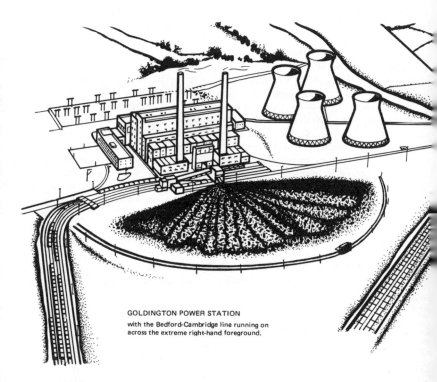

GOLDINGTON POWER STATION
with the Bedford-Cambridge line running on across the extreme right-hand foreground.

2353, which was identical to Goldington's engines, was delivered to the British Electricity Authority, Tilbury. The two Goldington Barclays were used to shunt materials delivered by rail for the station's construction and, after generating commenced, one locomotive was put into use seven days a week bringing in coal from the connection sidings with B.R., up to 12,000 tons a week being handled.

When first supplied the two 14-in. Barclays were normal coalburners but the management decided to convert them to oil burning, a method of firing which they believed to be more economical. It was also thought that oil for the locomotives would be easier to store than coal especially as oil storage containers were already installed in order to provide fuel for igniting the power station's coal fired boilers. Other advantages, of course, are quicker boiler pressure raising, as oil-burning locomotives can attain full pressure in little over an hour whereas coal consuming engines need over twice as long; and, perhaps equally important in Goldington's case, improved safety, in that a driver's attention is not diverted from the track ahead through his being involved in manual firing operations. Accordingly both engines in turn were returned by Pickfords low loader to Andrew Barclays of Kilmarnock for conversion, the necessary equipment for each costing £650. Perhaps the most remarkable aspect of this conversion was its complete success for although quite a number of British steam engines have been modified to this method of firing, they have invariably reverted to coal, for one reason or another; whereas these oil-fired Barclays still survive today.

So successful were they, in fact, that a long-term policy of steam operation at Goldington has been adopted. Eventually this raised the question of spares. A new boiler was estimated at £6,000, a figure deemed to be too high, and after some considerable searching the Goldington engineers were able to purchase for only a few hundred pounds an identical locomotive which lay in a semi-derelict condition a Blisworth, thus providing a good set of spares, and the boiler from this engine was re-tubed and given a new firebox by Anglo-Swedish for only £4,000. In the 1960s A.B. No. 2353, the original Tilbury engine, was acquired from Bow Power Station and this engine's boiler was fitted to ED9. Furthermore, both ED9 and ED10 were sent back to Kilmarnock in the mid-'sixties for complete overhauls at a cost in excess of £3,000 each. So it may be seen that by a process of careful overhauling and cannibalisation the station had been able to maintain two completely reliable engines – ostensibly the two which were purchased in 1954. Certainly a great deal of money has been spent on steam and certain district engineers proposed dieselisation upon several occasions, but genuine doubts as to the reliability of diesels thwarted such proposals, especially after the 100 per cent proven dependability record offered by these Barclays.

Quite apart from operational suitability I did detect at Goldington some degree of sentimental regard for steam and it proved to be a sentiment which went back much further than operations at Goldington. In fact it went back to the very beginning of steam itself and became personified in the naming of ED10 *'Richard Trevithick'*. So often we wonder what story lies behind a locomotive's name and although in some instances there is little to tell, many fine tales of engine names do exist, as in the case of these Andrew Barclays. It turned out that the station superintendent's wife was directly related to Richard Trevithick of Cornwall, the pioneer of the first steam engine, and some of his possessions have passed on into the superintendent's family. Hence the interest in the station's engines and the commemorative naming of ED10. It is furthermore proposed to name ED9 *'Matthew Murray'* – after another early engineer and associate of Trevithick.

Trevithick pioneered two locomotives in South Wales in 1804, one being the famous winner of the £500 Pen-y-daren prize, and although this locomotive was unsuccessful on account of the track, it was the first locomotive to haul a load successfully. The following year another of Trevithick's locomotives was put to work on Tyneside. He was a pioneer with high pressure steam whenever he could obtain wrought iron for the boilers, and he experimented with pressures of up to 100 lbs per sq. in. with some of his stationary winding engines. In 1808 Trevithick fired the country's imagination by constructing and exhibiting a passenger locomotive on a circular track in London and it is by remarkable coincidence that one of Bedford's leading chemists, who are an old showground family, also had connections with this demonstration in London. Trevithick was always greatly admired and his name has now acquired a legendary status.

Matthew Murray started where Trevithick left off and will be remembered for equipping the three-and-a-half mile long Middleton Railway in Leeds with a steam engine in 1811. This was by far the most successful engine up to that time. It had cylinders of 9 in. × 22 in. and drew a 94-ton train at $3\frac{1}{2}$ m.p.h. The Middleton Railway now exists in preserved form and steam engines operated by enthusiasts still run over this historic route. Such are the stories behind locomotive names and so may be understood the special endearment to Goldington of these modern counterparts of those halcyon days at the dawn of the nineteenth century.

In contrast with Trevithick and Murray's pristine machines these sturdy $29\frac{1}{2}$-ton Barclays represent an ultimate in standardised building policies over many years and their relatively moderate dimensions combined with a 5 ft 6-in. wheelbase within a total length of 23 ft made them eminently suitable for secondary duties in all facets of industrial use. No less than 306 examples of this basic 14-in. type have been built being used in collieries, gas and electricity plants, steel works, large private companies and government departments. Along with Barclays' larger 0–4–0ST and 0–6–0ST types this classic shape has predominated in British industry for over half a century. The dimensions are: cylinders 14 in. × 22 in., driving wheels 3 ft 5 in. diameter, boiler pressure 160 lbs per sq. in., grate area $9\frac{1}{2}$ sq. ft, total heating surface 542 sq. ft and tractive effort 14,300 lbs at 85 per cent of boiler pressure. It is interesting to note a comparison with their 16-in. 0–4–0ST relations in which the comparable tractive effort is 19,610 lbs (see page 103).

I clearly remember my visit to Goldington. It was one sunny day in the Autumn of 1971 when ED9, *Matthew Murray* to be, was performing operations. I felt that my picture needed to superimpose one of the Barclays onto the power station's splendid structures and it is worthwhile to note the almost impressionistic effect of the swirling smoke and steam intermingled with this industrial backdrop to which the autumn sunlight adds a stimulating warmth of colour. I think perhaps that Monet, the French Impressionist, would have loved this scene.

Should one perchance travel the ex-Midland main line on a sunny day the flat eastern landscape just south of Bedford will be seen to be dominated by such colours, and thoughts will doubtless be evoked of the little Barclays with which the station has been inextricably bound up for some quarter of a century.

Yorkshire Engine Co. Workhorse 0–6–0ST   Plate Nos. 9, 33

It was not without a considerable degree of elation that I received an invitation to Clipstone Colliery, Nottinghamshire, to film the final working hour of the last example from a class of lesser-known industrial locomotives. Clipstone Colliery, which is one of Britain's most productive, is situated five-and-a-half miles north-east of Mansfield, and concurrent with my visit the local *Chronicle* carried a column headed 'N.C.B. puts its faith in Clipstone' stating that the colliery was aiming for an annual output of $1\frac{1}{4}$ million tons. The subject of my attentions, however, was Yorkshire Engine Company 0-6-0ST No. 2521, a survivor from a breed of some fifty engines whose rough, chunky outlines seem to epitomise a sturdy workhorse. It is interesting to note that a carthorse was the trading symbol of the Yorkshire Engine Company. Bedevilled by a plethora of ailments, the engine went about its final duties, and when I was greeted by the N.C.B.'s Area Engineer he informed me that the engine was scheduled to go by low-loader the following day to the N.C.B. museum at Lound Hall, near Retford, where it was to be restored by apprentice engineers. He told me something of his long struggle to get the engine preserved, especially after his first choice, a Peckett engine, had virtually been cut up before his eyes, and I sensed the pride he felt in his eventual success in preserving one of the Nottinghamshire Coalfield engines. Plate 9 was made as the engine was bringing its last rake of wagons through the colliery yard and it provides a suitable epitaph for these fine locomotives.

The Yorkshire Engine Company of Sheffield were well-known locomotive builders for over a century, but in order to find the origins of these engines we must turn to the Newcastle works of Robert Stephenson, for it was from here that the first eight examples were built in 1936-7, followed by a further five in 1938 under R.S.H. – following Stephenson's merger with Hawthorn Leslie. These thirteen engines were specially built by Stephensons for the expanding Appleby Frodingham Steel Company at Scunthorpe – a part of the United Steel Group – and in design they are not dissimilar to a set of 18-in. short-wheelbase 0-6-0STs built by Stephensons in 1934 for United Steel's Workington Works. In passing, the Workhorses are also very similar to a 16-in. 0-6-0ST produced by Chapman & Furneaux of Gateshead in 1901, although I very much doubt that this engine was part of the same lineage.

The outbreak of war in 1939 caused production of the class to cease and none was built over the wartime period. Immediately after the war, United Steel acquired the Yorkshire Engine Company, and consequently when Appleby Frodingham required more of the class they were ordered from within the Group. Thus in 1945 new engines were ordered and deliveries commenced in 1947, the engines being known at the Yorkshire Engine Company as 'Stephenson Pattern Type

1'. Deliveries continued up to June 1954 when the last engine was delivered to Appleby Frodingham's Ore Mining Branch. Over this latter period of construction, thirty-eight examples came from Yorkshire Engine Company's works. Seventeen went to Appleby Frodingham's Scunthorpe Works and thirteen to their neighbouring Ore Mining Branch, whilst six went to other companies within the United Steel Group such as the United Coke and Chemical Company. Of the remaining two, one was delivered to the Lancashire Steel Company's famous works at Irlam, whilst the other went, of all places, to Peru! Although the Workhorses are now extinct in Britain, this last engine, Y.E. No. 2511, which was exported in 1952, still survives on shunting duties at the port of Lima on the Ferrocarril Central del Peru (FCCP). She is an oil burner and represents one of a number of steam exports which the Y.E. undertook to South America. Some detail differences occur between the Stephenson and Y.E. locomotives, the most noticeable being the straight-backed bunkers on certain Stephenson engines. All Y.E.s had angled ones.

The leading dimensions for the class were: cylinders 16 in. × 24 in., boiler pressure 180 lbs per sq. in., driving wheels 3 ft 8 in. diameter, grate area 16 sq. ft, total heating surface 859 sq. ft and tractive effort at 75 per cent boiler pressure 18,850 lbs. Their total weight in full working order was 52 tons, including a coal capacity of $1\frac{1}{2}$ tons, whilst the total length was $30\frac{1}{2}$ ft, height 11 ft 8 in. and wheelbase 11 ft 0 in.

Quite a number of Workhorses were named and they became a popular standard type throughout the Appleby Frodingham complex for some twenty years until the diesel era began to make itself felt throughout British industry. Accordingly, just three years after the last Workhorse had been constructed, United Steel at Frodingham took delivery of the first of a large fleet of Y.E. 0–6–0 D.E.s which during the late 'fifties and early 'sixties ousted the Workhorses, with the result that many passed into N.C.B. service in various parts of Britain.

Number 2521, although bearing a 1952 worksplate, was actually despatched from Y.E.'s works on 6 May 1953, whereupon she became Appleby Frodingham Steel Company No. 9. So she worked until being sold under the diesel programme to the N.C.B. East Midlands Divison Clipstone Colliery in 1962, where she remained for ten years as N.C.B. No. 9, until withdrawal in 1972. Sister engine No. 2522 was also banished to the Nottinghamshire Coalfields and worked from Teversal, whilst another of the class could be found at Gedling.

Considering the class's relatively confined existence, preservation has been considerable, for apart from No. 2521 at Lound, two other examples are retained. One of the R.S.H. engines, No. 6947 of 1938, is now on the Foxfield Light Railway, whilst another of the Y.E. examples, No. 2498 of 1951, may be seen at Quainton Road. These two locomotives ended their working days at Gedling Colliery, Nottinghamshire, and Chislet Colliery, Kent, respectively.

R.S.H. 18-in. 0–6–0ST   Plate No. 21

This engine is one of the most magnificent still in British industrial use, its basic design dating back to the time of the Hawthorn Leslie Company prior to their merger with Robert Stephenson. Ever since the early part of this century, Hawthorn Leslie had been building a large number of 0–6–0STs with outside cylinders, known as the Kersley class, and after the merger this basic type was continued with 16-in., 17-in. and 18-in. cylinders along with driving wheel diameters ranging from 3 ft 8 in. to 3 ft 10 in. The first example produced under Robert Stephenson and Hawthorn was for the Holmside and South Moor Coal Company in 1938, but owing to the outbreak of World War II and R.S.H.'s consequent involvement in manufacturing munitions, it was not until the early 1950s that the series appeared in great numbers. Altogether some seventy locomotives were built subject, of course, to slight variations at the purchasers' special request. Those supplied to the National Coal Board in Northumberland and Durham had either 17-in. or 18-in. cylinders and the type played an important part on such well-known colliery systems as Philadelphia and Ashington and became one of the most distinctive shapes in the latter days of steam in north-east England.

The locomotive illustrated was one of the 18-in. examples and was built as R.S.H. No. 7944 in 1957. When new she went to East Cramlington Colliery as N.C.B. No. 48, but later was transferred to Bedlington Colliery and was renumbered No. 62. After dieselisation had forced the engine into store at Bedlington it was moved on 1 October 1971 to Backworth, where after a further renumbering it became No. 16. At Backworth it joined two sister engines of the 17-in. variety, Nos. 44 and 47, and these engines are discussed on page 117+18.

In 1971, when the colour plate was made, No. 16 had become the last example of its kind. As a class these 53-ton engines constituted one of the most powerful industrial types ever built in Britain and although these engines had to be given time when starting away with heavy loads, they very quickly 'dug their heels in' and their massive free-steaming boilers ensured an excellence of performance on all heavy duties. Accordingly the type was popular with engine crews who, apart from appreciating the class's adequacy of power, also found their large roomy cabs praiseworthy. This latter virtue must have been a blessing, for the cab design of most industrial engines could hardly have been said to be congenial, in fact in many older engines it was extremely primitive! I always associate these 18 × 24-in. R.S.H.s with the three huge Hudswell Clark 18-in. 0-6-0STs built for the Manchester Ship Canal in the 1950s, the two types being remarkably similar in appearance, although the likeness is almost certainly coincidental.

At 85 per cent of its 180 lbs boiler pressure, No. 16 can develop a tractive effort in excess of 26,000 lbs, and this renders her rather more powerful than the Hunslet Austerities, largely because of the driving wheel diameter of 3 ft 10 in. against the Austerity's 4 ft 3 in. In fact, this tractive effort is greater than that of a class such as the ex-L.M.S. 4F 0-6-0s, which were main line freight engines, so dispelling a freqently-heard myth that industrial locomotives are always puny little things in comparison with main line locomotives.

During 1972 No. 16 was hard at work on Backworth's network where it was an especially attractive engine on account of its black livery, fine gold lettering and red side rods, whilst the bold inscription 'NATIONAL COAL BOARD', is much to be preferred to the more customary 'N.C.B.' (see plate 47). Because of badly worn flanges, No. 16 is not permitted to work to Fenwick Colliery as this involves crossing B.R. metals. Consequently, the engine is nowadays employed in taking trainloads of shale – waste products from the washed coal – up to the disposal point one mile north of Eccles Colliery (see map, p.112). Backworth's total weekly yield of 9,500 tons of saleable coal incurs the additional handling of some 4,000 tons of shale per week, and the sight of this engine storming northwards from Eccles Colliery with heavy shale trains was one of the typical Backworth scenes in the early 1970s.

I have included a map of the Backworth network as it was in its last days because this system, although much reduced from its former years when it included a line down to Whitehill Point Staithes on the River Tyne, is important in being steam's last stronghold in the north-east; for these historic coalfields were the very cradle of steam in the early 19th century. It is doubly appropriate that the plates dealing with Backworth should depict locomotives from Robert Stephenson and Hawthorn, because this company was founded by none other than Robert Stephenson himself in 1823. This was the world's first locomotive building company and it dates back to a time when the first steam locomotives of the world were appearing on Britain's north-eastern coalfields.

Backworth itself is steeped in coal mining history, the initial shaft having been sunk in the first half of the nineteenth century, and the whole surrounding area has since been extensively mined, both by open cast and deep mining methods. Over recent years only two pits have been operative, Eccles and Fenwick, and the steam engines are housed, maintained and deployed from the depot alongside Eccles

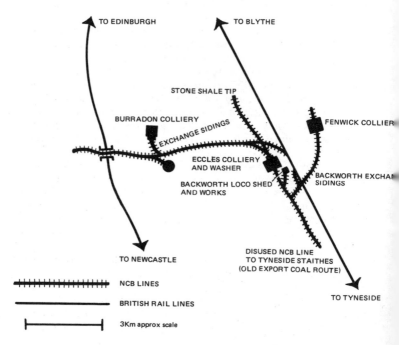

THE BACKWORTH COLLIERY NETWORK AT THE END OF STEAM.

TO EDINBURGH

TO BLYTHE

STONE SHALE TIP

BURRADON COLLIERY

EXCHANGE SIDINGS

FENWICK COLLIER

ECCLES COLLIERY
AND WASHER

BACKWORTH LOCO SHED
AND WORKS

BACKWORTH EXCHA
SIDINGS

TO NEWCASTLE

DISUSED NCB LINE
TO TYNESIDE STAITHES
(OLD EXPORT COAL ROUTE)

TO TYNESIDE

NCB LINES

BRITISH RAIL LINES

3Km approx scale

Colliery where a labour force of seven drivers and firemen, three fitters, two boilersmiths and one chargehand come under the direction of a locomotive foreman. This team cover motive power operations all round the clock. The map shows how the loaded coals are conveyed from the washeries of each colliery and marshalled into sets of various grades at the B.R. sidings situated midway between the two colliers.

For many years to come Backworth will be remembered for its associations with steam and coal, and over my many visits there I have always become conscious of the men's pride in their tradition, along with their determination to keep the engines going. Many of the older hands have entertained me for hours with tales of locomotives both past and present, tales which, when told by some of these hardy north-eastern men, become transcribed into some of the most poetic lore of the steam age. On several occasions I have sat around the eternally roaring fire in the depot messroom listening to tales enriched with an amazing combination of ethereality and earthiness and yet somehow, when I leave Backworth, the magic disappears and I can barely remember what has been said. As in the myth of the eternal fountain, one has to go there for oneself to sample the magic.

R.S.H. Austerity 0–6–0ST   Plate No. 26

This dawn study at Eccles Colliery on the Backworth system in Northumberland shows one of the ubiquitous Hunslet Austerities, of which some 300 were built for the Ministry of Supply during the latter part of World War II. These engines proved to be immensely successful and building continued after the war both for the War Department and for private industry. In fact it was not until 1964 – almost twenty years after the war – that building ceased and by this time a total of 484 engines had been built, no less than seven private locomotive builders having been involved in the Austerities' construction. Today they are Britain's most common steam type, over 100 still being operative in various collieries throughout the country. This particular engine was one of a batch of thirty built by Robert Stephenson and Hawthorn in 1943, originally numbered 7098 but being renumbered 75062 on delivery to the War Department. Altogether R.S.H. built ninety engines of this kind during the war and only two afterwards, both in 1953.

Like many Austerities, this engine has had a varied existence, as after the War she was released by the M.O.S. and in 1946 went into private industry, to the Bennerley Opencast Disposal Point, Nottinghamshire. After a year or so the engine moved northwards to the Bluebell Opencast Coal Workings in Northumberland, until a further transfer in 1959 took her to Backworth, where she became N.C.B. No. 49. Currently one of Backworth's several active Austerities, No. 49 is in use ove five days a week, and the engine's fine condition, the result of a complete overhaul at Backworth Works in 1971, has ensured that she is now in the hands of Backworth's senior driver. These engines are very popular at Backworth and No. 49 is scheduled to remain in operation for several more years, owing to the colliery's policy of standardising with locomotives of this type.

The Austerities' historical outline was covered in *Twilight of Steam* (page 136), whilst the type is further discussed in this volume on page 93.

R.S.H. 0–6–0T No. 31 Plate Nos. 37, 43

Of the many different designs of locomotive found in British industrial environments, the saddle-tank has been by far the most numerous, to such an extent in fact that side-tank engines have always tended to make a rather refreshing change. This is in marked contrast with many other countries where side-tank engines are far more prevalent. One of Britain's most prolific builders of industrial loco-motives was Robert Stephenson and Hawthorn (R.S.H.), of Newcastle upon Tyne, who in their later years of steam engine building produced a number of side-tank designs. Perhaps the best known of these were the outside-cylinder 18-in. engines which worked at Nechells, Hams Hall and Meaford Power Stations, the two engines from the last-named place now being preserved in America.

One of the company's lesser-known types is represented by the locomotive illustrated: National Coal Board No. 31 from Whittle Colliery, Northumberland. No. 31 is one of a small batch of powerful inside-cylinder engines introduced after World War II. These engines were confined to the coalfields of north-eastern England and immediately before nationalisation of the coal industry in 1948, the type could be seen working for the Horden Colliery Company Ltd, whilst in later years others worked at Wearmouth and on the famous Ashington Colliery network. The precise origin of the design is in some doubt, although certain authorities claim it to be a side-tank version of the renowned Hunslet Austerities, but I find some distinct resemblance to a 17-in. Hudswell Clarke design of the 1920s. However, in proportions these fifty-ton R.S.H. tanks are similar to the Austerities, both types having cylinders of 18 in. × 26 in., although their boiler pressures of 180 lbs per sq. in. are slightly greater than in the case of the Austerities (170 lbs per sq. in.), as are their driving wheels of 4 ft 6 in. diameter (against the Austerities' 4 ft 3 in.). It is the smaller wheel diameter of the Austerity which gives it a slight advantage in tractive effort – 23,870 lbs, compared with 22,540 lbs. In fact one of the principal characteristics of these side-tanks is their 4 ft 6 in. wheels which are exceptionally large for an industrial locomotive.

The engine illustrated was built at R.S.H.'s Forth Bank Works, Newcastle, in May 1950 and along with two sister engines was sent to Ashington, where they became Nos. 29, 30, 31 (R.S.H. Nos. 7607, 7608 and 7609) respectively. Because of their large driving wheels they gained a reputation for fast running and Ashington used them for operating workmen's passenger trains over the colliery network as well as for inter-colliery coal train workings. After dieselisation of Ashington in the late 1960s, No. 31 was transferred up to Whittle, whilst No. 29 went to Backworth, both transfers taking place in 1969. The same year rendered these two locomotives sole survivors of their kind owing to the premature scrapping of the Horden and Wearmouth engines and after No. 30 from Ashington had been cut up after succumbing to the miserable fate of colliding with a diesel.

No. 29's future at Backworth was destined to be far from happy, for although this has always been a completely steam-orientated centre possessing every possible facility for maintenance, this engine, I was told, nearly put them off steam for life. In the words of one Backworth official, and I understand his intuition, 'you know a bad design when you see one'. He was right, for the fitters soon began to complain about the dreadful inaccessibility of the inside cylinders, motion and oiling points, and plate 43 shows the narrow opening in the side tank through which the men had to work. Complaints came also from the loco crews who found the high spectacle glasses in No. 29's cab impossible to look through because of their height above the cab floor. Accordingly the engines had to be driven with the driver looking outside the cab – a method of operation strictly against N.C.B. regulations. This culminated in the Backworth crews' refusing to work the engine until the cab floor was raised to make possible proper use of the spectacle glasses. Design faults like these are remarkably obvious ones and it is odd that such engines should be built by so renowned a firm as R.S.H. Not surprisingly No. 29 was withdrawn in December

1971 and was promptly cannibalised in order to keep the ever-ailing No. 31 in service at Whittle – an engine whose fortunes were destined to be equally unhappy.

Apparently No. 31's peculiar shape had done little to inspire confidence at Whittle and the engine spent some time stored. Her rusty smokebox testifies to these periods of dormancy and to all intents and purposes the engine was withdrawn until a serious motive power shortage necessitated her use again in 1971 when, despite a number of chronic ailments, partly owing to a lack of fitting facilities at Whittle, the engine was pressed into service. During No. 31's working life at Whittle she was involved in an accident when a rake of runaway wagons hit the engine broadside and knocked it off the track. The enginemen miraculously escaped injury in the resulting avalanche of wagons, though damage to No. 31's framing necessitated heavy welding and this can be seen beneath the engine's smokebox on plate 37.

By the summer of 1972, No. 31 had developed bad leaks from both boiler stays and foundation ring, causing the engine to pour water out by the gallon. Furthermore, despite several repairs to a fracture in the steam chest, steam continued to ooze out alarmingly. Such behaviour hardly made the engine popular and, as one frustrated driver told me, 'it's a race to get the work done before the engine empties its water all over the track'. 'No easy matter,' he continued, 'because you can't see where you're going for steam!'

During our conversation he gave me some startling calculations, claiming that the diesel then being hired from B.R. at £25 per day was much cheaper to operate than a steam engine. Admittedly his assessments were part of his lighthearted 'anti-31 propaganda', but he claimed that the $2\frac{1}{2}$ tons of coal used on an eight-hour shift, costed at 17s. per cwt saleable value, combined with several 1,200-gallon tankfuls of water at domestic tariff, amounted to some £80 per shift – £160 over the two daily shifts – whereas the diesel's hire charge plus fuel was only half this figure.

Whether economically viable or not, a diesel's appearance at Whittle meant the beginning of the end for one of Britain's finest industrial lines, as the branch from the colliery up to the B.R. east coast main line was almost five miles long, set amid lovely Northumberland countryside. Despite all its shortcomings I became especially attached to No. 31. It was an affection which extended further than that normally bestowed upon last survivors, for in this essentially north-eastern type I found much interest and regarded its ugly chunkiness as being aesthetically pleasing – though I do admit that without the cutaway side tanks the engine would look rather like the matchbox that one engine driver insisted it was! Plate 43 shows No. 31 with a gnarled lineside tree, and an interesting pair they make, the tree possibly counterbalancing No. 31's austere lines.

R.S.H. 17-in. 0–6–0ST   Plate No. 22

On 26 November 1971 this locomotive, N.C.B. No. 47, was transferred on loan from Backworth to Whittle to cover an acute motive power shortage, and the plate depicts the engine a few days after its arrival. No. 47 is one of the last working examples of a Robert Stephenson and Hawthorn 17-in. 0–6–0ST design derived from the earlier Hawthorn Leslie Kersley class (see page 110), and it represents a type of engine commonly found on the north-eastern coalfields during the 1950s and 60s. The engine was delivered new to Backworth in 1955 having been built at R.S.H.'s nearby Newcastle Works, and she had the special distinction of being constructed as an oil burner, a rare experiment amongst British industrial locomotives and one which in this instance caused innumerable operational problems – solidification of the oil being one example. The following year saw its conversion to traditional coal burning, largely because 1956 was a year of oil shortage caused by the Suez Canal troubles, although the engine had performed so miserably in its oil burning state that eventual conversion back to coal was a foregone conclusion from the beginning. One other engine of the same class was similarly treated.

With the oil burning phase over No. 47, along with other members of the class, became very popular and they undertook many of the heavier duties over the Northumberland coalfields. These engines have been a familiar sight at Backworth for almost twenty years. One complaint however concerns their brasses in both the side-rods and big end, as these are in constant need of attention. Otherwise, in the words of a Backworth fitter, 'they knock like a bag of hammers'. Another interesting point about these locomotives is their flangeless centre driving wheels for traversing sharp curves; this is rather unusual on an engine having a wheelbase of only 11 ft 6 in. Leading dimensions of the class are: cylinders 17 in. × 24 in., driving wheel diameter 3 ft 10 in., boiler pressure 170 lbs per sq. in., and total weight 45 tons in full working order.

In 1966 No. 47 underwent a major overhaul in the N.C.B.'s area workshops at Ashington and, along with another Backworth engine of the same kind, N.C.B. No. 44, it was still in action in 1972, by which time these two engines had become the only survivors. The loan of No. 47 to Whittle was part of a motive power policy at Backworth of centralising all steam operations on the commoner Hunslet Austerities of which the system had several (see plate 26). This in fact was part of a wider N.C.B. policy of concentrating the last steam engines north of the Tyne at Backworth, and in these final years of steam power it was felt that the problems of maintenance and availability of spare parts could only be overcome satisfactorily with a standardised fleet. Of course, in the British industrial scene of the early 'seventies the Austerity was the obvious contender. This meant that Nos. 44 and 47 and their 18-in. relation No. 16 became somewhat outlawed. At the time of writing none of these 17-in. engines has been earmarked for preservation although the almost identical No. 16 is almost sure to be saved (see plate 21).

The plate shows the handsome silhouette of these classic north-eastern industrials as No. 47 heads a coal train along the five-mile branch from Whittle Colliery to B.R.'s east coast main line. The wintery sky makes an evocative backdrop to this December scene.

Andrew Barclay 15-in. 0–6–0ST   Plate No. 47

Shortly after the miner's strike in 1972 the B.B.C. televised a documentary entitled 'A Month of Sundays' depicting the life and culture of Shotton, an ancient Durham mining village. The village's heartbeat was of course its colliery and the programme highlighted the miners' lives – the bitter-sweet existence of rugged men whose every day was night. Shotton is a village steeped in history and to the visitor it appears as a living example of a nineteenth-century mining community with its long rows of stark terraced cottages lining criss-crossed streets, all dominated by the colliery which looms up like some demoniac temple. Certainly the village is relatively untouched by modern times but amongst its dankish environs one feels a spirit of neighbourliness and welcome – for here is a place where the inhabitants toil together and because of their familiarity with hard times and tragedy they are blessed with that exquisite sociability which is so absent from our modern communities.

The people of Shotton were proud of their community even if many hated the pit, and when the news came that the seams of coal which had spread out for miles around the village were running out and the colliery was to finish it seemed inevitable that the village would die. On account of the pit's impending closure Shotton had for some years been regarded as a dying area and few improvements were made, much to the bitterness of Shotton's inhabitants.

Shotton, which was the first of the Horden Colliery Company's pits, was sunk way back in 1833 and was one of the pioneer pits of County Durham. For the social historian Shotton offers a great deal but it possessed another distinction, this one of interest to locomotive enthusiasts, for this Durham backwater was appropriately host to England's oldest steam engine in daily commercial service. The engine concerned was Andrew Barclay No. 1015, a priceless 34-ton 0-6-0ST dating back to 1904. This engine had worked in the area all her working life having been supplied new to the Horden Colliery Company and it was one of the very few six-coupled Barclays ever to work in the north-east of England.

When I made my pilgrimage to Shotton in order to film No. 1015 I found the engine to be a living testimony to over seventy-five years of classic Barclay shaping and this engine is so wonderfully characteristic of its maker that some consideration must be given to its lineage. Andrew Barclay & Company began building industrial locomotives in 1859 and over the following century some 2,370 steam engines originated in the company's Kilmarnock Works. Barclays have always been a family company and have never really expanded past this. Emphasis has always been upon quality – the firm never having indulged in mass production techniques. Barclays pioneered the fireless locomotive in Great Britain in addition to serving a very wide export market, but in Britain the company became especially noted for its range of four- and six-coupled saddle-tanks, engines which became famous for their style and longevity. Upon analysing this style, one will note the dominant features of rounded outside cylinders, square sides to the saddle tanks and the absence of a rear coal bunker. These aspects may clearly be seen on the plate of No. 1015 which also possesses the attractive curved cab sheeting characteristic of many turn-of-the-century Barclays. Another feature well illustrated by the plate is the forward extension of the saddle tanks, in very marked contrast to many saddle tanks from other builders who often left an exposed smokebox so giving their engines an entirely different aura. Even when other builders did extend their saddle tanks over the smokebox, they invariably gave them rounded sides instead of Barclay's squared ones and on account of this the engines looked completely different. Thus we readily notice that unmistakable Barclay front.

Other typical Barclay features are their thick chunky spokes and wheel rims and attractively-shaped sandboxes which stand on the engine's running plate above the cylinders. Looking at these aspects on the plates one can instantaneously assimilate the main features of the rugged Barclay look and a comparison of plates 51 and 42 will show how over the years chimneys became shorter whilst saddle-tank fronts became deeper. Barclay's chimneys were creations of no small distinction. Compare the almost obscene flower-pot style of the Polkemmet engine – see plate 51 – with No. 1015's solidly-built but vintage air. Many later engines had the shorter, robust ones as epitomised by plate 42. It is fascinating to see the many slight variations in all these basic ingredients of Barclay's wide range of 12–18-in. saddle-tanks. The Shotton example which had 15 × 22-in. cylinders was one of Barclay's first 0–6–0STs and a total of twenty-three engines to this design were built for use in collieries and steelworks.

In 1961 No. 1015 took respite from duties at Shotton when she returned to Barclays for a heavy overhaul which included fitting a new steel firebox and tubeplate. These repairs took a year to complete. The plate was obtained in 1971 when the engine was in daily operation, and the scene depicts No. 1015 bringing a rake of empty wagons up to the colliery just before daybreak. Because of the engine's superb features I felt that it might best be appreciated against a veil of darkness and seconds after this picture was made the first blue streaks of dawn appeared over Shotton's western aspects. Also in 1971 almost identical looking Barclays of the 0–4–0ST type could be seen at Graig Merthyr Colliery near Swansea and at Yates, Duxbury & Sons' Paperworks at Heap Bridge, these engines dating back to 1906 and 1904 respectively.

The ending of 'A Month of Sundays' showed the miners returning to work after the strike and as if commemorative of this we saw the Barclay jubilantly puffing its way along the yard amid shrouds of steam. Here like a shimmering ghost was a piece of living history which only a few months later became a memory. The pit closed, the Barclay disappeared, and Shotton village reluctantly turned toward a new and unknown era. The face of County Durham was never to be quite the same again.

Hudswell Clarke 0–6–0T   Plate No. 35

Sugar railways are normally associated with tropical climates and one's imagination wanders to the little lines of Barbados or perhaps those on the Indonesian archipelago. Certainly few imaginations tend to wander to the sugar lines of Britain's East Anglia, for seemingly few people realise the extent of the British sugar industry. Since the widespread development of sugar beet growing during the present century the eastern parts of England have become famous for their yield of sugar, the finest area being from the Humber south to Ipswich. So vast is this industry that Britain now produces no less than 900,000 tons of white sugar per year – about one-third of the national requirement. Unlike the cane sugar from the tropics, Europe's home produced sugar comes from the sugar beet plant, a root crop looking rather similar to a swede, but whether it be from cane or beet, the extracted product is sucrose. The origin of this sucrose is unimportant as a fully refined sample of sugar cannot be associated with its plant of origin.

The sugar beet seed is sown in early spring and the September harvest is followed by the manufacturing season. Throughout the season, which lasts until the following January, Britain's sugar factories work all round the clock on what is known as the 'campaign'. Over these months some $6\frac{1}{2}$ million tons of beet are processed in seventeen factories. Obviously railways must come into such a mammoth undertaking and many sugar factories have their own railway systems. By 1972 the British Sugar Corporation's Peterborough factory had become widely known for its immaculate Hudswell Clarke 0–6–0T which, over the campaign, shunts immense loads of sugar beet around the yards. This is the engine illustrated in plate 35.

She was built in 1946 as H.C. No. 1800 – although the works plate registers her as 1947 – and she was supplied new to the British Sugar Corporation, Peterborough, for £4,600. The history of this type is really fascinating as it dates back to 1909 when Hudswell Clarke specially prepared the design as a 10-ft-wheelbase engine for the Burry Port and Gwendraeth Valley Railway. After the grouping of Britain's railways in 1923, this batch of engines was absorbed into Great Western stock taking numbers 2164–9. Subsequently they passed into British Railways ownership but all had disappeared by 1953.

Six years after these engines had been supplied to the B.P.G.V.R. Hudswell Clarke made some very small changes to the design and used it as a basis for a standard class which produced some eighty locomotives between 1915 and 1955. The principal difference between the two types was the centre access to the motion cut into the side tanks of Hudswell Clarke's standard engine. This was a marked improvement over the B.P.G.V.R. engines which had plain-sided tanks, and the loss of water capacity incurred by the cut-away sections was well compensated for by extending the tanks slightly forwards. This in fact increased the water capacity from 830 gallons in the original engines to 1,200 in the standard.

The first of these new standards went to the Port of London Authority who took no less than thirty of them between 1915 and 1954. Others were supplied to the Ministry of Munitions in 1918 and again in 1943 for use in steel works and docks, whilst large numbers went to the National Coal Board around 1948–9. It is interesting to note how these later engines had increased in price since Peterborough's engine was built, as those supplied to the N.C.B. in 1953 cost £8,300 each! Many engines of this kind remain at work today, especially on the Yorkshire coalfields, and although these particular engines are attractively painted red many have had their stylish Hudswell Clarke chimney removed in favour of a stovepipe one. Another splendid example may be seen at work on the scenic colliery branch at Shilbottle, Northumberland.

The Hudswell Clarke Company was founded in 1860 on land occupied by the famous 'Railway Foundry' in Leeds. Throughout its hundred years of steam building it was destined to concentrate upon industrial locomotives, which the company supplied to countries throughout the world, and it is hoped that some of these will be covered in later volumes of this series. Whilst mentioning Hudswell Clarke's exports, it is of interest to note that a locomotive named *Helgenas,* which was delivered to Sweden in 1889, is still working there, albeit in preserved form, though the amazing thing is that its boiler is the original one. I imagine that this 83-year-old veteran is probably the oldest working steam locomotive in the world retaining its original boiler.

However, to return to No. 1800, we find yet another case of an engine much loved by the crews and although the Peterborough factory has acquired a diesel, the campaign's intensity invariably necessitates the use of both locomotives. Rather strangely, the British Sugar Corporation have neither numbered nor named No. 1800 although she is unofficially named *Thomas* in commemoration of the Reverend Awdry's Thomas the Tank Engine – which she closely resembles. In fact she was named '*Thomas*' at an unofficial ceremony by Awdry himself and a face was affixed to the smoke box front. Had any of Awdry's younger readers seen the engine in this condition they would hardly have believed their eyes!

Apparently the face is still used occasionally but it had certainly disappeared when I went to Peterborough to film *Thomas* one snowy night in 1971. It was bitterly cold with a wind sweeping unmercifully across the tableland of eastern England. Upon entering the town around midnight I was greeted by the indescribably unsweet smell of sugar processing. This was the height of the campaign and *Thomas* was working all round the clock in view of the B.S.C.'s diesel having broken down. As a result, *Thomas*'s fire had not been dropped for over a week and so urgent was the situation that there was talk of steaming up the Hunslet 0–6–0ST *Jacks Green* which, although preserved by the Peterborough Locomotive Society, is stored on B.S.C. premises upon the understanding that the factory can use her in an emergency. Needless to say some of the employees were longing to steam up *Jacks Green*!

The crop is delivered to the factory from miles around by both road and rail, and evidence of the campaign may be seen in the sugar beet which lies on East Anglian roadsides after falling from the droves of lorries speeding it to the factories. So here, in the heart of Britain's least known industry, is this fine locomotive and never will I forget that exciting night when despite snow and cold, plus the terrible smell from the factory, I enjoyed the company of *Thomas* over several hours. It is intended that she will remain at Peterborough over many future campaigns and as the engine lies idle throughout the summer one imagines what a fine attraction she would make on the near-by Nene Valley Line, should the Peterborough Locomotive Society succeed in opening it up as a tourist attraction.

In common with all sister engines built from 1915 onwards No. 1800 has the following dimensions: cylinders 16 in. × 24 in., driving wheel diameter 3 ft 9 in., boiler pressure 160 lbs per sq. in., and tractive effort at 85 per cent boiler pressure 18,570 lbs. The engines have a total heating surface of 715 sq. ft and a grate area of 12.5 sq. ft. Coal and water capacities are $22\frac{1}{2}$ cwt and 1,200 gallons respectively, whilst the total weight in full working order is 42 tons.

R.S.H. 0–4–0ST 16-in.   Plate Nos. 18, 25, 61

Upon the nationalisation of the electricity generating industry in 1948, one of the problems besetting the newly-formed British Electricity Authority was the need to increase Britain's generating capacity, not only to overtake the wartime arrears of construction, but also to meet the ever-increasing demand for electrical power. As part of this development, work was put in hand for a £30-million station of 600,000-kilowatt capacity at Castle Donington in Leicestershire. The station was conveniently situated alongside the River Trent and was within easy reach of the rapidly expanding East Midland Coalfield. At the time of its construction Castle Donington was Britain's biggest power station and one of the largest in Europe. Construction work started in the early 1950s and, as many materials were delivered by rail, two of these 16-in. 0–4–0STs were ordered from Robert Stephenson and Hawthorn in 1954 to assist with the building programme before generating began. These engines, R.S.H. Nos. 7817 and 7818, were numbered 1 and 2 respectively. Generating commenced in 1956 and was brought up to maximum upon completion of the station in 1959.

At maximum generating capacity the power station can consume 42,000 tons of coal per week, and this arrives by B.R. in 1,000-ton trains, usually hauled by a Peak class diesel. It is the duty of these 0–4–0STs to split up these trains and convey the coal from the sidings which connect with B.R. down to the automatic waggon tippler, from which the fuel goes by conveyor belt to the station's boilers. The locomotives then return these empties back to the departure sidings for B.R. to collect. Altogether the power station possesses some ten miles of railway sidings.

It is interesting to note that the station also owns two Andrew Barclay diesels, but despite this steam is normally in operation. This is not because of an enthusiastic preference for steam, as in some industrial establishments, but simply because of its much greater reliability, and here is yet another case of industrial management admitting that, when reliability is essential, steam power is to be preferred, notwithstanding its higher operational cost. Thus it is Castle Donington's official policy to retain steam in full working order for an indefinite period. Accordingly, a great deal of money has been spent in maintaining these two locomotives, both mechanically and externally. Furthermore the management believes that clean and properly maintained locomotives will be all the better respected by the operating staff.

The engines have steel fireboxes for longer life whilst copper ferrules are fitted between the tubes and firebox to eliminate leaks. Over recent years Castle Donington's status has fallen somewhat. It is no longer a base load station generating round the clock and accordingly only one loco is now in use over two shifts per day. However the engines are cleaned weekly and washed out fortnightly whilst the station chemist regularly takes water samples from the locomotives' blow down valves to ensure freedom from scale, so protecting the boilers' lives, as high acidity content in the water can cause serious corrosion. Even the coal burnt by the engines is carefully chosen. Thus it will readily be appreciated that Castle Donington's staff are doing everything possible to ensure the internal cleanliness of boiler and firebox so vitally important to the longevity and efficiency of a steam engine. With such care lavished on them these two R.S.H. 0–4–0STs are as perfect mechanically as any in British industry. In 1971 No. 2 went to Warren Brothers of Newhall, near Burton-on-Trent, for a major overhaul and it is the Generating Board's intention to treat No. 1 similarly later in the 1970s.

The colour plates depict No. 1 at work during the winter of 1971–2 and plate 18 shows the wonderful livery conceived by the station superintendent. Certainly one would not like to see all locomotives painted so garishly but these engines do make a refreshing change from the grime of many industrial locomotives – see plate 51. In contrast plate 61 illustrates a singular aspect of the beautiful Leicestershire countryside, amongst which the power station is set. No. 1 achieved fame when it was chosen to appear in the D. H. Lawrence film *Women in Love,* the engine having been specially adorned in period attire to represent a turn of the century colliery shunter. During the making of this film No. 1 was driven by Castle Donington staff on B.R. metals some miles away.

We must now look briefly at the history of this design, in order that it may be seen in perspective, because these engines are a standard 16-in. 0–4–0ST, typical in shape and styling of a range of other 0–4–0STs by R.S.H., with 12-in., 14-in. and 15-in. cylinders and coded by R.S.H. 'Munition', 'Kitchener' and 'Stella' respectively. This basic 0–4–0ST shape dates back to the Hawthorn Leslie Company long before their joining up with Robert Stephenson and Company. Vast numbers of engines have been built to this basic pattern over the last sixty years or so, and it is fascinating to see how this characteristic Hawthorn Leslie shape has been perpetuated in the newer company. Notice especially the saddle tank and dome shapes, inclined rounded cylinders, and styling of cab and side sheeting, along with the location of sandboxes above the cylinders and behind the rear axle. Such facets come together in a robust design which is thoroughly pleasing to the eye and one which has become an intrinsic part of the British industrial scene. One of the R.S.H. 12-in. Munition engines adorns the cover of *Twilight of Steam* and this engine's basic outline may be readily compared with that of No. 1. The dimensions of these 16-in. engines are: 2 cylinders 16 in. × 24 in., driving wheel diameter 3 ft 10 in., boiler pressure 160 lbs per sq. in., and tractive effort of 18,160 lbs at 85 per cent of boiler pressure.

With two such delightful examples of the steam age permanently in traffic, Castle Donington has become a focal point for enthusiasts from all over Britain, whilst preservationists have also earmarked these engines. But seemingly they will have to wait a long time, for almost certainly these two 0–4–0STs will be amongst the very last steam engines to work in British industrial service. Another engine of the same type, named *Mars,* worked at Leicester Gas Station and this is destined for inclusion in the Leicester Museum of Technology, whilst similar engines of varying vintages may be found in preserved form at Grosmont, Quainton Road and Ashford, and on the Middleton Railway, Leeds.

Peckett 14-in. 0–6–0ST   Plate No. 4

Locomotive building commenced in Bristol in 1860 with the now legendary firm of Fox Walker. This company built prolifically over a twenty-year period until a serious reduction in business forced the works to close. Shortly afterwards Fox Walker's premises and drawings were acquired by Thomas Peckett and so began the firm which was to take a leading place amongst Britain's private locomotive builders – for Pecketts from their Atlas Works supplied locomotives to all facets of British industry and indeed to many parts of the world. About the time of Peckett's inception, one of Fox Walker's partners built up the neighbouring firm of Avonside and the combination of the two works made Bristol one of Britain's great locomotive producing towns. Nowadays it is remembered along with Stafford, Manchester, Leeds, Newcastle, Kilmarnock and Glasgow.

When I asked a friend his feelings about Peckett locomotives he immediately described them as 'refined' and here, in a word, he coined as good a generalisation about them as is possible. Peckett's engines have been noted over many years for their elegance and some of their best-loved features are their capped chimneys, smokebox wing plates – not much within themselves, but they make an immense difference to a locomotive's appearance – dome-mounted safety valves and distinctively curved saddle tanks which in the case of many larger engines were delightfully amplified by the delicate curvature of the engine's backplate and coal bunker. Such characteristics when added to an attractive livery and a liberal lacing of brasswork combine in a superb looking locomotive, and whilst quite a number of Peckett's creations were far more utilitarian in appearance, the vast majority possess a special air of refinement.

One of the last retreats for Pecketts in Britain is Brynlliw Colliery on the anthracite coalfield of South Wales and it was here that the plate was obtained. The engine illustrated is Peckett No. 2114 of 1951, a member of the company's B3 class with 14 × 22-in. cylinders, 3 ft 7-in.-diameter driving wheels, a boiler pressure of 180 lb per sq. in. and an $8\frac{1}{2}$ sq. ft grate area. Approximately twenty engines of this class were built between 1931 and the early 1950s and they were widely used by Fords of Dagenham. Brynlliw has two other Pecketts: one is an older B3 engine of 1933, whilst the other is an 0–6–0ST of the B2 class. These engines, which were a forerunner of the B3s, have 14 × 20-in. cylinders and were introduced in 1902. Both types look almost identical. Forty-three class B2s have been built, some for the Port of Bristol Authority, whilst others have seen widespread use in collieries. The fact that these two designs look almost identical demonstrates once again the minute differences which occur between various batches of industrial locomotives and also how engines are built to the same general shape over many years.

No. 2114 is a typical Peckett and it is fitting that she should be decked in an attractive green livery. The engine only arrived at Brynlliw in 1970 having been transferred from Morlais Colliery, Carmarthenshire, where she had lain idle for some time, and her transfer to Brynlliw made the colliery solely Peckett-operated, and so consolidated resources for spares. She is unofficially known as *Sir Winston,* a name bestowed in view of the engine's having taken part in the making of the film *Young Winston.* Understandably, Pecketts rate highly amongst preservationists and their character may also be seen in the North Norfolk Railway's 16-in. 0–6–0ST of the 0X1 class, whilst a similar 16-in. engine may still be found operating commercially at Merthyr Vale Colliery, Aberfan.

I felt that Brynlliw Colliery was the best place to film Britain's surviving Pecketts and I arrived there in torrential rain to find the grimy *Sir Winston* undertaking her duties. I was soaked long before I had found the engine shed, but a blazing fire therein, combined with a kindly offered mug of tea, did much to restore me. The men were very interested in their Pecketts and claimed that many people came to see them, whilst one engineman insisted most vehemently that all three were exactly alike! My visit to Brynlliw was during the overtime ban prior to the miners' strike of 1972, hence the engine's appalling external condition, and upon innocently remarking that such a condition hardly befitted the Peckett lineage – especially for colour filming – I was warmly invited to do the cleaning myself. There was however no shortage of volunteers to arm me with rags and paraffin. Very shortly I was up on *Sir Winston*'s buffer beam amid falling rain and the gathering gloom of dusk, desperately trying to make some impression. But the dirt was caked on like an armour and I mused that if it had been possible to clean the engine, the rain would have done it hours previously. Such impression that I did make may be seen on the plate, and though opinions of the result may differ, I have at least brought out the complementary hues of red and green, so providing the plate with a valuable contrast in colour.

The picture was not made until some hours after darkness because I waited for *Sir Winston* to come up from the B.R. sidings with a rake of empty wagons. The swirling images of her fire and steam reminded me of Turner's wonderful storm scenes and I thought how much he would have liked these heightened effects in contrast with the engine's shape and colouring. *Sir Winston* ambled past with a hissing and clanking, the glow of her fire turning the steam to a flickering orange inferno. The huge wagons rumbled past in the darkness and through a heavily falling rain I made my way back to the colliery. Another fragment of steam's magic had been captured.

Bagnall 0–6–0ST 'Victor'   Plate No. 34

The motor age and the steam locomotive can hardly be said to have common connotations, especially in 1972, but one of the most interesting locomotives in Britain may be found at work in a car factory. The locomotive is *Victor*, William Bagnall No. 2996 of 1951, and the factory none other than Austin's famous Longbridge Works.

Victor's origin is equally fascinating for it offers testimony to the many conflicting feelings in the steam *versus* diesel controversy which was rife throughout all facets of Britain's railways in the early 1950s. The truth is that Brush/Bagnall received an order to supply four 400-h.p. diesel-electric shunters in 1950 for the Steel Company of Wales at Margam. However, the Steel Company were not convinced about the total superiority of diesels and in view of the fact that Bagnalls had built steam locomotives for them, both before and during World War II, they took the step of specially requesting the building of three new steam engines blessed with as many modern sophistications as possible, in order that they could be compared in day to day service with the diesels. In this connection, it is fascinating to look upon Bagnall's advertisements for the early 1950s which ran 'Steam or Diesel? Many railways and industrial users are convinced that steam traction is still the most economical and conventient form of motive power. Bagnall's experience covers eighty years and we build both steam and diesel, accordingly we are able to give comprehensive and impartial advice to those in doubt as to which type is most suitable for their operating conditions.' Such is the plausibility of advertising, for it seems strange that a company of Bagnall's status should be unable to differentiate upon a question the answer to which had become a few years later a foregone conclusion throughout much of the world. The Steel Company's trials were scheduled over a lengthy five-year period to enable an accurate costing of maintenance and overhauls, an indication of the extent of the Steel Company's uncertainty on diesel traction at that time. In 1950 the first of these unique engines arrived – W.B. No. 2994 – to be followed in 1951 by W.B. Nos. 2995–6, British Steel numbering them 401, 2 and 3 respectively.

In order that they might compete favourably, Bagnalls equipped the class with many features not normally found on industrial locomotives: SKF roller-bearings on axles and motion, outside Walschaerts valve gear and piston valves – in spite of the engines being non-superheated. These factors alone rated the class well above the standard of engine prevalent in industry, but this was not all for, in common with many main line engines of the day, they were given rocking grates and self-cleaning smokeboxes. Also incorporated were hopper-type ashpans, Lambert wet sanding gear and Owen's balanced regulators. What a contrast they made with many of their almost centenarian industrial counterparts and to Bagnalls goes the credit for producing this *pièce de résistance* in British industrial engines.

As the reader will anticipate, the trial's outcome went in favour of diesels and after the five-year period Brush/Bagnall received an order for seven 360-h.p. diesel-electrics. By 1957 the three '400 tanks', as they were known, became surplus to requirements and Nos. 401 and 3 were sold to Austin Motors, Longbridge, in September of that year, whilst No. 402 went to the N.C.B. in South Wales, where she worked at various collieries including Ogilvye and Groesfeem. By April 1967 this engine had ended up at Birds Commercial Motors where, it is said, an attempt was made to fit an ex-G.W.R. Pannier Tank boiler to her. Presumably by this time No. 402's original boiler was in need of considerable attention. However this gallant attempt failed and she was cut up later the same year.

Better futures awaited her two sisters however and after arrival at Longbridge their numbers – 401 and 403 – were removed and replaced with the respective names *Vulcan* and *Victor*. Their duties here consisted of moving such materials as coal and oil into the works, along with conveying loads of new cars down to the B.R. exchange sidings as shown by the colour plate. These new cars are loaded onto special bogie carflats from the platforms of the adjacent disused B.R. station at Longbridge. This line was once part of the Midland Railway's Halesowen branch.

Longbridge's use of locomotives like *Vulcan* and *Victor* may be better understood when the factory's tremendous appetite for fuel is considered; each year it consumes 92,700 tons of coal and over 8 million gallons of oil. Car manufacture began on the site in 1905, when Herbert Austin established the Austin Motor Company – a firm destined to become the largest of the British Leyland Motor Corporation's 60 factories. Nowadays, Longbridge covers 290 acres and employs 25,000 people, and it has a capacity for producing 9,000 vehicles, 5,000 bodies, and 23,000 engines per week! In fact it is a city within itself and may be compared in terms of population with such towns as Newarke-on-Trent and Yeovil. Longbridge is currently producing nearly half of British Leyland's output of over a million vehicles per year and its importance in the national economy is likely to continue growing.

Longbridge has been noted for its locomotives over many years, Manning Wardle/Hunslet 0–6–0STs in the earlier days, but these huge Bagnalls are by far the most famous. Note their chunky, powerful appearance, outside steam pipes and straight-sided saddle tank – a typical Bagnall hallmark, see plate 29. So interesting are these locomotives that in May 1970 *Vulcan* was chosen for display at Tyseley's steam exhibition along with many ex-main line engines, and an immense amount of interest was taken in her.

By 1972 *Vulcan* had fallen into disuse and it was rumoured that *Victor*'s days were also numbered. Accordingly I made a journey to Longbridge in the winter of 1972. The works face the wooded Lickey Hills and are an industrial output of Birmingham's south-western boundary. As I walked through the heavily populated ferment which surrounds the works I could hear *Victor's* superb chime whistle screaming and echoing like a banshee. The huge engine made a striking sight, completely dwarfing the new cars and vans which stood in their hundreds all around her. It was almost incomprehensible to see a steam engine amid such motor-mania.

The engine crews hold *Victor* in very high esteem and she is kept in immaculate condition, a special touch being her red-painted valve gear which looks especially attractive and makes a fine contrast with the green livery. The men are fully aware of *Victor's* uniqueness and hope to keep her in use for as long as possible, but when she is finally retired it is to be hoped that either she or *Vulcan* will be preserved, as these highly unusual and sophisticated engines constitute perfect examples of steam's rearguard during those crucial years of decision in the 1950s.

Andrew Barclay 18-in. 0–6–0ST   Plate No. 51

Nowadays the name Polkemmet conjures up a great deal in the minds of steam enthusiasts for in this West Lothian colliery can be found the finest assortment of vintage industrial locomotives in Britain, including the country's oldest working engine. This celebrity is N.C.B. No. 8, Andrew Barclay 0–6–0ST No. 885 of 1900, and the plate shows her in fine contrast with Polkemmet's ex-War Department Austerity – a Hunslet-built engine which the N.C.B. purchased from the W.D. for £1,500. It is fascinating to note that there is no less than forty-three years' difference in age between these two locomotives.

No. 8 is a veteran in the truest sense and although she has had a chequered career the engine's seventy-two years of working life have all been spent in Lanark and West Lothian. In October 1900 Andrew Barclay supplied the engine to John Watson Ltd, Eddlewood Colliery, near Hamilton, Lanarkshire, whereupon she was named 'Eddlewood No. 3'. Only two engines of this type were ever built, the other being supplied to the Lanarkshire Steel Company, Glasgow. Their cylinders of 18 in. × 24 in. and 3 ft 8 in-diameter driving wheels rendered them one of the largest engines built by Barclays up to that time whilst certainly they were the first 18-in. engines the company ever built. After building these two saddle-tanks Barclays fitted their standard 18-in. engines with side tanks (see plate 32). After the closure of Eddlewood Colliery around 1920, the locomotive was transferred to one of the Company's other collieries at Robroyston, near Stepps, where it worked until 1932, whereupon a further colliery closure resulted in the engine being sold to William Dixon's Calder Iron-works, Glasgow, in 1934. The engine is believed to have worked for part of 1934 at Calder Ironworks before being transferred to Dixon's Colliery at Polkemmet, where it became Polkemmet Colliery No. 14. Upon the nationalisation of the coal industry on 1 January 1947 the engine passed into N.C.B. ownership and under a later renumbering scheme became N.C.B. West Lothian Division No. 8 of Polkemmet Colliery.

In 1972 Polkemmet possessed five steam engines, the other three being an A.B. 0-4-0ST of 1904, an A.B. 0-6-0ST of 1924, which at the time of my visit was employed as standby engine, and a dismantled Grant Ritchie 0-4-2ST of 1917. In common with Barclays, Grant Ritchie also had their works at Kilmarnock and their designs were often very Barclay-oriented, both companies producing 0-4-2STs with remarkable similarities in appearance. This wheel arrangement was quite unusual but it did enable relatively large engines to be built onto a short coupled wheelbase.

Apart from Polkemmet having Britain's oldest steam engine it is also one of the few places where double heading is regularly employed. Such operations are necessary as the climb from the colliery yard up to the B.R. exchange sidings on Polkemmet Moor is very severe – requiring that two locomotives be put vigorously through their paces. I was fortunate to find No. 8 working in tandem with the Austerity and was especially pleased that No. 8 was the leading engine. This was because the older engine's gravity sanding apparatus is deemed to be more reliable than the steam-operated equipment on the Austerity. Such a matter is unimportant on dry days but if a shower of rain wets the rails there exists a danger that the trains will slip to a standstill if adequate and fully reliable sanding arrangements are not provided. However my visit was made one sunny May morning and I arrived soon after sunrise in order to see the daily complement of eight loaded trains go up the bank. Only one shift a day was operative, the first train going up about 7.00 a.m. and the last in the early afternoon. The trains consisted of some twelve loaded waggons totalling about 300 tons and the sight of these two engines storming the bank constituted what was for me Britain's greatest steam spectacle. The method of operation was that both engines stood in the colliery yard at the foot of the bank with their fires well made up, issuing palls of smoke across the surrounding landscape – a habit which does little to endear these historic machines to the local residents, especially on

Mondays! Once a loaded train was ready both engines were opened up in an all-out assault on the gradient. By positioning myself on the side of a huge slag heap I obtained a fine view of the bank, and it was from here that the illustration was made. The Austerity created a steady, even blast whilst the ancient lady in front wheezed and rasped away in a totally different rhythmic pattern, so creating a marvellous polyphony of sound. Spellbound, I spent many hours watching this performance during which time I was treated to a footplate trip on No. 8 up to the exchange sidings on the edge of Polkemmet Moor. This is a fascinating bracken and heather covered wilderness situated amid a skyline of colliery tips and industrial embroilment.

Understandably there was some affection for No. 8 at Polkemmet but this did not extend as far as cleaning her, neither for that matter was anyone induced to clean any of the other engines there. Herein lies another Polkemmet distinction – its unfailing ability to maintain the grimiest set of steam engines imaginable! There is an obvious virtue in the attainment of cleanliness but so dirty are Polkemmet's engines that one comes to see a virtue in the attainment of sheer grime. It was hard to believe that underneath those solidified black layers lay a beautiful shade of green. Mechanically, however, things were much happier and No. 8's lively performances were partly due to her having been given a completely new boiler by Barclays in 1961 – even as late as 1972 Barclays were still prepared to supply spares for steam locomotives. Apart from her new boiler, the Polkemmet shed staff insisted that No. 8 was exactly as built, with the sole exception of her chimney which had to be cut down 6 in. when the engine arrived at Polkemmet in order to get into the shed. Perhaps this incident has something to do with the chimney's wonderful flared shape.

Despite a great difference in age between No. 8 and the Austerity – almost forty-five years at the drawing board stage – their dimensions and weights are remarkably similar, the Barclay having cylinders of 18 in. × 24 in., 3 ft 8 in.-diameter driving wheels, a boiler pressure of 160 lbs per sq. in. and a total weight in working order of 45 tons, compared with the Austerity's 18 × 26-in. cylinders, 4 ft 3 in. diameter driving wheels, 170 lbs pressure and total weight of 48 tons.

Despite the antiquity of Polkemmet's steam fleet – five engines totalling 277 years of age – it appears that no plans are in hand to dieselise and one hopes that this paradise of steam will continue. Certainly in the summer of 1972 plans were in hand to have No. 8's wheels completely retyred as they were badly worn and would not allow a further turning up – not an operation to be undergone if the engine faced imminent withdrawal. It is heartening that so fine a spectacle as the Polkemmet workings can still be enjoyed in Britain, especially with such fascinating engines, and it seems that this West Lothian colliery is destined to enjoy fame for at least a few years to come.

FINLAND

Finland's Railways date back to 1862, a time when the country was a Grand Duchy of the Russian Empire. Despite this, locomotive development has always taken an independent line and, although the 5 ft 0 in. gauge conforms to the Russian one, Finland's locomotives form a rather unique and conservative family, the vast majority being simples with two outside cylinders and a minimum of mechanical sophistications. The first locomotives were obtained from England and America and it is from the latter country that some of the most attractive features of Finnish engines have derived, namely the huge spark arresting chimneys, cow catchers, and warning bells.

This distinctive family of locomotives owes much to the development of Tampella and Lokomo Oy – two large engineering companies who since the early part of this century have been responsible for building the majority of Finnish steam locomotives. Tampella, founded in 1861 by the rather unusual merger of an engineering works and a linen mill, have built engines for the state railway since 1900, whilst Lokomo Oy was founded fifteen years later for the manufacture of locomotives. Over the years the two companies have worked in close co-operation, both being based in Tampella, an industrial city rather inappropriately referred to as the 'Manchester of Finland'.

Although a considerable range of types has been built, the family lineage is always apparent, perhaps being personified in the excellence of cab design. The cabs are extremely commodious, possessing two side windows and ideally-placed controls, whilst virtually all latter-day engines possess air-operated foot pedals facilitating automatic opening of the firehole doors during firing. Because of Finland's severe winters the cabs are, of necessity, almost totally enclosed and extra warmth is obtained by sliding heavy duty sack-cloth curtains over a bar situated in the cab roof. Other standard characteristics are round-topped fireboxes, parallel boilers with two domes, and two-toned

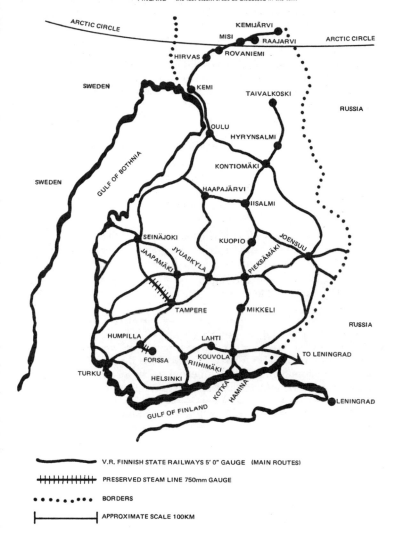

FINLAND — the last steam areas as discussed in the text

ARCTIC CIRCLE

KEMIJÄRVI
MISI
RAAJARVI
ARCTIC CIRCLE
HIRVAS
ROVANIEMI
SWEDEN
KEMI
TAIVALKOSKI
RUSSIA
OULU
HYRYNSALMI
GULF OF BOTHNIA
KONTIOMÄKI
SWEDEN
HAAPAJÄRVI
IISALMI
SEINÄJOKI
KUOPIO
JOENSUU
JYUASKYLA
JAAPAMÄKI
PIEKSÄMÄKI
TAMPERE
MIKKELI
RUSSIA
HUMPILLA
LAHTI
TO LENINGRAD
FORSSA
KOUVOLA
RIIHIMÄKI
TURKU
HELSINKI
KOTKA
HAMINA
LENINGRAD
GULF OF FINLAND

V.R. FINNISH STATE RAILWAYS 5' 0" GAUGE (MAIN ROUTES)

PRESERVED STEAM LINE 750mm GAUGE

BORDERS

APPROXIMATE SCALE 100KM

whistles, which form the basis of a rather complicated communication code. All the locomotives featured in this volume are superheated.

During the construction of Finland's Railways extensive areas of bog and clay were encountered which made the building of stable road beds both difficult and expensive. Consequently very light rails were used resulting in inevitable restrictions upon axle loadings and speed. Although the V.R. has done much track upgrading over the last decade, much of the network is still railed at 90 lbs per yard and even less. So it will be understood that locomotives are thought of largely in terms of axle weight rather than in terms of wheel arrangements. As shown in the following table, the capital letter in a class code indicates the locomotive's duty and the smaller letter its axle weight grouping.

H	—	Passenger
P	—	Suburban
S	—	Mixed Traffic
T	—	Freight
V	—	Shunting

k	—	locos with an axle loading up to 11 tons
v	—	locos with an axle loading up to 14 tons
r	—	locos with an axle loading in excess of 14 tons

The figure gives guidance on the age of the class, the oldest being 1. Thus Tk3, for example, indicates the third marque of a freight engine with up to 11-ton axles.

The Finnish landscape is an exciting blend of lakes and conifer woodlands. The country possesses some 60,000 lakes whilst over 70 per cent of the land is covered in forest. Thus the use of wood as locomotive fuel has been widely adopted. As the colour plates show, birch is predominant amid the pine and spruce forests and owing to its high calorific value it became the favoured form of fuel. However, timber products form a very important part of the Finnish economy and since 1948 the Finns have found it cheaper to burn imported Russian coal rather than their native birch, which has of recent years become increasingly significant in the manufacture of paper and associated products. Because of this, wood burning on locomotives had largely died out by the start of the 1970s, although a large number of engines fortunately retained their spark-arresting chimneys and some, especially the Tk3s, still burned a mixture of coal and logs in 1972.

The fitting of cow catchers is essential in view of the fact that the majority of the V.R.'s route mileage is through wild, unfenced country. These cow catchers are known as 'reindeer catchers' in the southern part of Lapland, and during the winter of 1970 there were no less than eighty incidents reported of locomotives striking reindeer over the 51-mile run between Rovaniemi and Kemijärvi (see the map on page 135). All classes have the air-operated warning bells. These are lovely to hear and are frequently used around stations, especially where no passenger footbridges or subways exist. In contrast with such a precaution it is amazing to note that Finland's steam locomotives are painted in a rather unusual shade of conifer green and as such they almost completely merge with the enveloping woodlands. Certainly this creates a perfect aesthetic blend with the landscape but one would have thought that it could hardly be conducive towards general safety. However the Finns have more than made up for any such anomaly with their Hr12 class of diesels which are painted red and cream with bright blue cigarette advertisements along the side of the engine!

Industrial expansion in Finland, combined with the V.R.'s dedication towards continually improving its already excellent services, has meant a rapid rundown of steam power and although as recently as 1950 almost all traffic over the V.R.'s 3,000 route miles was steam-operated, the early 'seventies saw its virtual elimination from all main line services and its relegation to either shunting or operating P.W. trains in connection with track maintenance and upgrading. In 1972 the steam stock had dwindled to a mere 258 engines, many of these being stored as stand-bys, although representatives of ten different classes could still be seen in action. Only seven years earlier the V.R. possessed over 500 steam engines.

One heartening aspect is Finland's policy of storing steam engines in full working order for a possible crisis, and many such engines, representing seven different classes, are already placed. On a different note, the attitude taken towards preservation is a highly enlightened one and apart from the prolific contents of the National Railway Museum, locomotives of several types are stored on public view in various parts of the country, as instanced by the superbly restored Tk3, which is mounted alongside one of the main platforms at Kouvola.

By 1972 one enthusiast-operated line was providing steam services for tourists during the summer months. This is the 15-mile 750-mm-gauge line from Forssa to Humppila run by an organisation called 'The Friends of the Steam Locomotive', who use a rather attractive 2–8–2T. Perhaps more endeavours in this direction might follow; certainly the V.R. authorities are aware of the tourist possibilities of steam and in this superbly run country very little seems to be ignored which is of proven value. Finland has already become the final outpost of steam in Scandanavia and this is a situation which is expected to last until the mid-1970s.

V.R. Tv1 class 2–8–0   Plate Nos. 1, 30, 36, 40

The 2–8–0 type has always played an important part on Finland's railways ever since its inception there in 1900 with the twenty U.S.A. Baldwin-built Tk1s and it became the most numerous type in the country. There were two principal classes: the Tk3 Little Jumbos which are discussed on page 142, and these, the more powerful Tv1 class, appropriately known as Jumbos. Originally classified k3, these engines have an axle loading of 13.1 tons and a tractive effort of 32,739 lbs at 85 per cent boiler pressure. With the exception of the much later Tr1/Tr2s these were the most powerful freight engines Finland ever had. (Some later Tv1s, which had boiler pressures of 185 lbs per sq. in., had a tractive effort of 35,470 lbs.) They were needed when loads became heavier in accordance with Finland's industrial expansion and the class became widely employed in the south where the track was heavier. It may be said that the Tv1s precipitated the introduction of the Tk3s because a more powerful engine was needed to take these heavy trains when they were transferred from heavy to lighter rail, as the older Sk1 and 2 and Tk1 and 2 classes previously used on these duties were becoming increasingly strained.

The Tv1s have plate frames and as such may be regarded as the last engines of the earlier period of Finnish design, all subsequent classes having bar frames. It was in the rigidity of their plate frames that one of the class's principal weaknesses lay, as these were prone to cracking, and although reinforcement work was carried out it rendered them stiffer than before. This problem beset the class over much of its life, as did the Jumbos' habit of breaking their front-end side rods at high speed (caused by their Krauss bogies). One of the design's most prominent features was the forward situation of the dome and herein lay another potential source of trouble because when the engines were running in reverse there was a danger of water surging forwards in the boiler and entering the steam collection pipe. The minimum danger from this was excessive priming, whereupon sooty water was rather unceremoniously ejected from the chimney, but more serious was the perpetual fear of water entering the cylinders in sufficient volume to cause piston and cylinder block fractures. One wonders why the dome was not relocated on later examples, especially as Tv1s were built over a 28-year period. Such problems aside, the Tv1s were extremely fine haulers, capable of handling trains of up to 1,000 tons, and the class acquired a reputation for their ability to operate heavy freights over long and tortuous gradients. For these reasons they became Finland's second most numerous class.

The first ones appeared from Tampella in 1917 and by 1945, when the last examples were built, ninety-seven had originated there. Between 1923 and 1936 twenty-five engines came from Lokomo Oy and the total of 142 was made up by ten each from Hanomag of Germany and Nydquist & Holm of Sweden, in 1923 and 1928 respectively. Finland has never been an exporter of locomotives, but five new Tv1s were sold by Tampella to Latvia during the 1920s as a payment for linen – it was noted earlier that Tampella also had considerable linen interests. Rather remarkably, one of these engines came back to Finland from Russia some twenty years later amongst a batch of returned war reparation locomotives, Russia having gained control of Latvia in the interim period..

Many of the class were wood burners and of course had huge spark-arresting chimneys, but all latter-day engines are coal burners fitted with slender stovepipe chimneys and in this form they remind me very much of the S.N.C.F. 140C 2–8–0s of the same period (see *Twilight of Steam* plate 10). Plate 30 shows clearly the ash-chute underneath the smokebox. This is a standard fitting on Finnish locomotives and it avoids the need to open the smokebox door to remove ash. Notice also the neatly shaped wooden box on the running board; this is a characteristic Finnish innovation for carrying tools. By the early 1970s only a few Tv1s remained, many of their duties having been taken over by Sv12 diesels.

One of the Jumbos' last haunts is Kontiomäki, a small village in north-eastern Finland important only as a railway junction. In the early spring of 1972 I spent several days in Kontiomäki to see these engines in action. Normally they were confined to shunting duties but at the time of my visit one of them was involved in the conveyance of sand from Hyrynsalmi, near the Russian border, to Kontiomäki, in connection with permanent way work on the Kontiomäki to Joensuu line, and so one morning I made the trip with engine No. 921 built by Tampella in 1936. We left Kontiomäki at 7.20 a.m. and proceeded northwards, light-engine, to collect our train load of sand. It was a day of rippling sunlight and blue skies as we drifted through an endless array of conifer woodlands interspaced only with lineside villages and the occasional lake. During the journey I learnt that No. 921 was carrying the boiler it was originally built with in 1936. Usually boilers are freely interchanged between members of a particular class during overhauls, for if reconditioned boilers are available when a locomotive enters the shops it greatly speeds up the shopping process. In fact, 921's boiler had been fitted onto two other Tv1s, but by remarkable coincidence the engine had received its original one back at its last overhaul. The trip produced some moments of uninhibited excitement as we raced northwards on a trip which reminded me of certain epic scenes in Walt Disney's *Great Locomotive Chase,* our Jumbo literally rattling, rolling and bouncing along its light trackbed, and during the height of this gallop I was ushered over to the driver's side to be shown the crater left by a Russian bomb during World War II.

Having reached Hyrynsalmi, the engine went down to the quarry to collect its train of sand whilst I waded waist deep in snow to obtain plate 36. As I was to find out, the Tv1s really are fine pulling engines, but the lightness of their axle load causes them to get into trouble through slipping and when No. 921 attempted to lift its 35-wagon train out of the pits it stalled dramatically, sending palls of exhaust up into the frosty air, more akin to a hydrogen bomb than a steam locomotive. After several attempts to start, each becoming more dramatic than the previous one, it became evident that other methods must be sought, whereupon we all shovelled sand from the trackbed onto the rails for some 30 yards in front of the engine. After more fireworks we finally pulled back onto the main line with the wheels still spinning dizzily. Had we stalled again it would have meant splitting our 600-ton train and undertaking some rather complicated shunting movements.

In the course of the 29-mile run back to Kontiomäki, our 98-ton Jumbo was required to surmount long gradients but throughout speed was maintained with the control settings ranging between half and full regulator at 30 per cent cut-off. One point which did surprise me was the long distances we rolled with steam completely shut off and on one occasion we ran for several miles at 30–40 m.p.h. without the slightest wisp of steam. There is an exhilaration about footplate riding which cannot easily be communicated by words, but that journey through the sunny and snow-covered Finnish landscape lives poignantly in my mind. The ever-changing textures of the smoke from white, to grey, to black, the gurgling roar of the Friedmann injector, the clanging shovel and flash of vivid orange as the firehole door opened, along with the flickering needle of the pressure gauge, are but a few of the magical elements which combine to produce steam's universal appeal.

As we ran into Kontiomäki, sister engine No. 923 was engaged upon shunting duties and I was reminded that this little village was the last retreat of these fine engines. Another three miles brought us to the permanent way works whereupon gangs of men proceeded to empty our wagons, (plates 30, 40). One hour later we propelled the empties back to Kontiomäki yards and after taking coal and water, No. 921 retired to the shed leaving me to watch the delights of No. 923 on shunting duties. By the day's end I felt I had made a really fine acquaintance with the Jumbos.

Rather strangely, no Tv1s are scheduled for preservation – a peculiar omission when one considers their importance in Finnish locomotive history, although it is possible that one of the military reserve engines will be retained in the distant future. One hopes so, for it is no consolation to say that if a Tv1 is seen again on Finnish metals it will be in a time of national crisis.

The class's leading dimensions are: cylinders 22 in × 25½ in., boiler pressure 171 lbs per sq. in., increased in some engines to 185 lbs per sq. in., 4 ft-7 in. driving wheel diameter, and grate area 25 sq. ft. Total length of locomotive is 58½ ft and the coal and water carrying capacities 5 tons and 3,523 gallons respectively. The total weight of engine and tender in full working order is 98 tons.

V.R. Tk3 class 2–8–0   Plate Nos. 8, 19, 20, 41

Looking back into locomotive history we find that perhaps the best loved of the classic types was the early American balloon-stacked chimney locos with their adornments of cow catchers, bells, brass lamps and tenders piled high with logs. Herein lies the intrinsic personality of Finland's Tk3 class and as such they create a living analogy with their Walt Disney-style counterparts of today, conjuring up memories of the old Wild West engines which still race through the depths of our imaginations. What a fine sight these woodburning engines make amongst the conifer-dominated landscape of Finland, like iron dinosaurs devouring the surrounding vegetation. Clearly the Tk3s' shape derives from early American engines and the class bears more than a superficial resemblance to the Baldwin-built Tk1s of 1900.

141

Appropriately known to the Finns as Little Jumbos, the class was prepared for lightly laid lines which had a rail weight of 45–50 lbs per yard and as such was intended to replace the earlier and less powerful Sk1 2-6-0s and Tk1/Tk2 2-8-0s. The Tk3s have an axle loading of 10.7 tons and are permitted to haul trains of up to 880 tons. So successful were they that the type quickly spread to all parts of the country and became used on a wide variety of duties including some local passenger working in the Helsinki area.

The class was first introduced in 1927 and building continued until as recently as 1953, by which time a total of 161 had been reached, thus making them Finland's most numerous class. The great majority were built for the V.R. by Tampella and Lokomo Oy, the first ones coming from Tampella's Works in 1927. Over the ensuing twenty-one years, Tampella produced eighty-two examples whilst Lokomo Oy, who built the final ones in 1953, constructed a total of fifty-nine engines, also from 1927 onwards. The remaining twenty came from A/S Fricks of Aarhus Denmark in 1949 and 1950, owing to the fact that the two Finnish works were busily engaged in producing narrow gauge steam locomotives for Russia as a result of the reparations treaty after World War II, under the terms of which, Finnish industry was obliged to supply Russia with various industrial commodities. In fact, the Finns also ceded one-fifth of their territory to Russia, which contained 17 per cent of their railway network at that time. Included were a number of TK3s and it is believed in Finland that some of these are still in use in Russia today. The locomotives illustrated are both of the Fricks batch, as indeed were most of the survivors in the north-eastern part of Finland during the early 1970s.

Originally classified K5, the class has bar frames, piston valves and Walschaerts valve gear, all being standard features in latter-day Finnish practice. Many, but not all, were wood burners although it was quite commonplace to convert engines according to current demands. Conversion to wood-burning is relatively simple and basically only involves removing the brick-arch and fitting the spark-arresting chimney. This wood-burning chimney is equipped with a kind of propeller whose rotary motion creates a vortex which extinguishes the sparks and causes them to fall down into the smokebox. Plate shows one of the Fricks engines which has been converted to coal-burning and it is intriguing to note what an immense difference the slender mesh-covered chimney makes to the locomotive's outward appearance when compared with the otherwise identical engine in Plates 19, 20.

All the V.R.'s coal burners had additional meshes situated inside the smokebox.

The Tk3s' comparatively small size makes them ideal shunting/ tripping engines and it is in these duties that they are ending their days, the northern towns of Oulu and Kemi being especially noted as their last haunts. In 1972 over thirty members of the class had been stored in full working order as general purpose engines in the event of a crisis – a fact further bearing out the class's all round versatility. No less than three have been preserved. One is for the railway museum at Helsinki, whilst another is intended for a local museum at Pieksämäki. The third example, the most exciting of all, was preserved by railwaymen and adorns one of the platform ends of the ultra-modern station at Kouvola, so creating a fascinating contrast in railway development. At the time of my visit to Finland in 1972, fifty-seven Tk3s remained in traffic, including all the Danish-built ones.

The leading dimensions of the class are: cylinders 18 in. × 24¾ in., driving wheel diameter 4 ft 2 in., boiler pressure 199 lbs per sq. in., grate area 17 sq. ft and tractive effort 27,530 lbs at 85 per cent of boiler pressure. Their atractive outside-framed six-wheel tenders hold 4.5 tons of coal and 2,090 gallons of water, whilst the total weight of engine and tender in full working order is 78 tons and their combined length 53 ft. Officially their maximum permitted speed is 40 m.p.h. My first experience of a Tk3 was very early one morning at Oulu. It was an idyllic day with the sun shining from a cloudless blue sky. As I made my way down to the station I could see wisps of smoke rising high into the frosty air, for there to greet me was a shining green Tk3 engaged in shunting duties and plate 20 was made during that morning as the engine assembled sets of wood panelled coaches for a Helsinki-bound express. This illustration shows clearly the raised silver numerals on the engine's cabside and I regard this as the finest style of locomotive numbering I have yet encountered.

Later on my tour I was lucky enough to find a balloon-stacked sister engine summoned out for snow clearance duty at Rovaniemi after a particularly heavy storm and I was in fact invited to help light up the engine. This was done by throwing eight 2-ft-long birch logs into the empty firebox, after which a blazing log was added. A further ten logs were thrown in and this was sufficient to kindle the engine's fire. Several hours later, after a few more rounds of logs, the engine had sufficient steam to leave the depot. One of the loveliest aspects of these wood burners is the sweet woody aroma which emanates from them, this being especially noticeable as they amble by. Plate 8 shows this locomotive, No. 1163, later that evening in Rovaniemi yards and in this picture I have tried to epitomise some of the essence of Finland's ambience by fusing its most characteristic locomotive type with the falling snow on a backcloth of distant conifers.

V.R. Tr1 class 2-8-2 Plate No. 3

When looking back over the final years of steam one finds that many countries adopted a standard type which represented their ultimate so far as steam traction was concerned. Finland was no exception, its finale being reached with the production of two designs, the twenty-two famous Hr1 Pacifics built between 1937 and 1957 and these sixty-seven mixed-traffic Mikados of type Tr1. Completely Finnish in design, these classes came at a time when main line tracks had been upgraded sufficiently to take their axle loadings of 17 tons. The boilers of the two types were interchangeable and both classes looked remarkably similar, possessing many common characteristics including identical windshields and cab design, whilst additionally both had bar-frames and large eight-wheeled bogie tenders. Because of the early dieselisation of all express passenger services, the Hr1s had a very short life, nineteen of the twenty-two being stored away by the army as early as 1971. Of the remaining three one was destined for Finland's National Railway Museum whilst the other two, which were the last active examples, lie out of use at Mikelli, much to the disappointment of local enginemen with whom they were immensely popular. Fortunately the same fate did not befall the Tr1s, the class being intact in 1972, and although many are stored or assigned to standby duties it is still possible to find them at the head of 1,300-ton trains of timber, cellulose and agricultural goods. This figure represents their normal maximum permitted tonnage but over level routes they take trains of almost 1,500 tons.

Despite their modernity, the Tr1s possess a superb elegance and are pleasing to the eye in every respect. As I became more familiar with them they became increasingly attractive, to such an extent that I now rate these engines as one of my greatest favourites. Functionally one must rank them with such types as B.R. Standard 5, S.N.C.F. 141R, R.E.N.F.E. 141F, D.B. 050 and the J.Z. 06, but aesthetically the Tr1s have a classic aura completely lacking in these counterparts of other lands.

It was in the troubled times of 1940 that the first Tr1 emerged from Tampella Works and only five were built prior to the advent of World

144

War II. The war delayed their construction considerably and building ceased altogether in 1943 after only thirteen engines had been completed. Until this time the Tr1s had been Finland's most powerful freight locomotive but in 1946–7, immediately after the war, the V.R. received by special purchase twenty 2–10–0s. Classified Tr2, these 17.5-ton-axle-loaded engines were American built by Alco and Baldwin and the V.R.'s batch was part of a much larger order destined for Russia. These immigrants were more powerful than the native Tr1s, their comparative tractive efforts at 85 per cent boiler pressure being 51,260 lbs and 45,830 lbs respectively, and so satisfactory were these Trumans, as the Finns called them, that tests were made in 1950 to decide whether to adopt these as Finland's standard freight type in place of the Tr1s. Eventually a choice was made in favour of the Tr1s, partly because they had the obvious advantage of boiler interchangeability with the Hr1s, and accordingly Tampella resumed building them again after a lapse of seven years.

After 1950, however, production really got under way and by 1956 a further eighteen had come from Tampella along with fourteen from Lokomo Oy. Also during this period twenty were commissioned from Jung of Jungenthal in Western Germany during 1953. The last two were delivered from Tampella in 1957 and the distinction fell on one of these, V.R. No. 1096, of being the last steam engine built for Finland's State Railways (Tampella Works No. 972). The final four Tr1s built, Nos. 1093–6, possessed some interesting differences from all earlier engines in that Tampella built them with roller bearings on all axles and connecting rod big-ends, along with small German-type Whitte smoke deflectors. It is amazing how these four engines differ in appearance through having smaller windshields, and in this modified form they look rather like a sophisticated version of the ex-Prussian 2–8–2s of 1922. It became customary for the V.R. to paint the motion of these roller-bearing engines red, giving them an extra touch of distinction, and because of their bearings these engines were employed on the fastest freight duties often involving speeds in excess of 70 m.p.h.

As the Tr1s made their debut on Finland's railway network, they began to replace the older Tv1/Tv2 classes which were becoming too slow and weak for the heavy and fast trains of the day. The class became known as Ristos, a name bestowed upon them in honour of Finnish President Risto Ryti who was in office when the first Tr1 was built. It was Finnish practice to name locomotive classes after presidents and other examples can be quoted such as Pekka, after Ukko Pekka, for the related Hr1 Pacifics and Hindenburg for the Hv3 4–6–0s. The Tr1's American 2–10–0 rivals of World War II were simply known as Trumans, and the Vr4s, later rebuilt to Vr5s, were called Little Trumans.

Many interesting characteristics can be found on the Tr1s such as their huge centrally-placed domes which contain sand, top-feed housing and the regulator. This makes a marked contrast with the traditional Finnish practice of having two domes. Their gaunt chimneys are often topped with wire mesh spark arrestors although some engines have these fitted at the base of the chimeny petticoat. But along with their cow catchers my favourite adornment is the locomotives' numbers set into illuminated panels on the main headlamp's side – not much within itself, but nevertheless adding greatly to the engines' appeal, especially when the numbers are lit up in gloomy or night time conditions. In common with some Hr1s the class is fitted with pressure equalising piston valves instead of the traditional by-pass ones, whilst their leading trucks are of the Krauss Helmholtz type. Some later engines were given welded steel fireboxes.

The class's leading data are: cylinders 24 in. × $27\frac{1}{2}$ in., boiler pressure 213 lbs per sq. in., driving wheel diameter 5 ft 3 in., grate area an adequate 38 sq. ft and total heating surface 2,103 sq. ft. Their huge tenders hold 9 tons of coal and 5,940 gallons of water, whilst the locomotive's total length is 73 ft. The size of these locomotives can be assessed from their total weight in full working order of 157 tons.

It would be no exaggeration to say that my affection for the Tr1s stems directly from a number of dramatic adventures I had with them, the foremost being an eight-hour footplate journey with an engineer's special from Rovaniemi northwards over the Arctic Circle into Lapland. It was winter, and we were scheduled away from Rovaniemi yards at 2.41 a.m. A swirling snowstorm was sweeping the town when the lights of Jung-built 1074 came into view as she approached the sidings to collect a string of empty ballast wagons. We were to take these empties up to Raajärvi quarries, some forty miles into Lapland, and return with a loaded gravel train for track upgrading work at Hirvas, south of Rovaniemi (see map page 135).

Chilled and covered in snow, I mounted 1074's footplate to find a cheery crew who seemed pleased, if a little surprised, that an English visitor should be joining them. Upon drawing out of the yards we entered a world of vivid extremes as from the hot, roaring locomotive one looked out on the cold arctic blizzard sweeping across the desolate, white landscape. Silent, green conifer trees slid past endlessly, being lit to a momentary brilliance by the cab's flickering orange glow. The roar of 1074's exhaust must have been audible for miles as the huge engine charged northwards like some anguished giant on the rampage. Seldom before had steam engines appeared so wonderfully exciting as on this incredible journey. Inside, the firing policy for 1074's 38-sq.-ft grate area was 'little and often', every shovelful bringing a blinding white-hot glare into the cab, followed instantaneously by the 'clang' of the air-compressed firehole doors closing. It is necessary to close the firehole doors between shovelfuls because apart from excess heat entering the cab, admission of cold air onto the firebox tubeplate amid such temperatures sets up stresses which considerably shorten its life.

Without warning our 2–8–2 suddenly slowed down, seemingly in the middle of nowhere, and the driver eagerly waving a powerful hand torch beckoned me over to his window. With the engine now slowed to a walking pace he shone the light out into the snowy blackness. After a time he found his target for there in the torch's beam was the Arctic Circle sign to which he enthusiastically pointed. It is at moments such as this that all language difficulties become totally resolved, man communicating freely with man. For many years I had wanted to visit the Arctic Region but never did I imagine that it would be in so dramatic a way as this.

Having entered Lapland, speed soon returned close to the engine's permitted maximum of 55 m.p.h., and I took a turn at firing, noticing as I did that the logs and coal on the tender were completely white with snow, whilst looking ahead the *Mikado*'s blazing headlamps showed the single track to be completely snowed over as ours was the first train over this lonely route for some hours. One gained the eerie sensation that we were no longer running on rails. After leaving Misi we turned south-eastwards down the branch to Raajärvi, where some hours were to be spend loading our train. Over the thirty-two miles from Rovaniemi to Misi we had climbed from 267 ft to 561 ft above sea level. From Misi the main line continues up to Kemijärvi and onwards into Russia, but since World War II the route has not been used as a crossing point.

During the wait at Raajärvi, Mauno, our fireman, demonstrated his way of making coffee by filling an ancient blackened kettle with water, hooking it onto the end of a fire pricker and extending it into the firebox. After boiling point was reached it was drawn out and some ten teaspoonsful of ground coffee were added, whereupon it was left to stew, along with a couple of huge Finnish skin sausages, on the Friedman injector mount. Later these were sampled by all and never did food taste so good as in this remote Lapland quarry.

Dawn broke as we returned towards Rovaniemi and Lapland's remote beauty impressed itself upon me. Reindeer tracks could be seen alongside the railway whilst the grip of winter rendered the innumerable lakes and rivers invisible, their presence only being indicated by a lack of trees. With a deep, throaty roar 1074 sped its heavy train southwards, flushing pairs of willow grouse from the lineside bushes and leaving inky black smoke trails across the sky. This fine locomotive's surging power was frustrated by the fact that we were on light rail and nothing greater than the authorised 55 m.p.h. was advisable. At 8.00 a.m. we rolled into Rovaniemi and even in this remote area the magic of steam was apparent – judging by the many people who paused to watch our train arrive. Perhaps their interest was accentuated by the comparative scarcity of Finnish steam, for 1074 was only on loan to the area to work these special engineer's trains.

A fortnight later I was lucky enough to have a footplate journey with the last Tr1 built, No. 1096, on the 5.10 p.m. freight from Pieksämäki to Kouvola, a distance of 115 miles. This train was one of the last main line steam workings in Finland and on this occasion consisted of ninety-seven axles making up a train of 900 tons. A week or two previously our engine had come out of Kuopio Works after overhaul and her condition was superb. The Tr1's riding qualities are excellent, whilst its cab layout represents the ultimate in Finnish steam practice and is one of the most congenial I have ever experienced. Of course the 5 ft 0 in. gauge does help in this respect! One notices the cleanliness, spaciousness and general orderliness of Finnish locomotive cabs, even the oil cans having the engine's number stamped on them.

I noticed that No. 1096 was worked at 30 per cent cut off and half regulator over much of the journey but as on my run on No. 921 (see page 139), there were long periods of rolling with steam shut off. However there were some fine bursts of speed especially over the newly ballasted sections when speed rose in excess of 60 m.p.h. During the run, I was assigned to blow 1096's whistle as we approached the innumerable level-crossings – Finland has about 8,000 of them! It had been my intention to return from Kouvola with another booked steam frcight later the same evening, but we were sidetracked so many times along our single line route that it became obvious that we would not reach Kouvola before the northbound train departed. The delay was largely due to our having to wait in loops for some special diesel-hauled 1,800-ton coal trains from Russia. Darkness had fallen by the time we were signalled into a remote loop some ten miles north of Kouvola and this I realised would be to allow the northbound steam train to pass. Having abandoned all hopes of catching it I resigned myself to the poor compensation of watching it hurtle past. The pant of 1096's Westinghouse Pump was the only audible sound amid the silent woodlands until through the still night could be heard the roar of an approaching steam train. Nearer and nearer came the throbbing rhythms of a two-cylinder steam engine until to my utter amazement and delight I realised that it was going to stop and, sure enough, sister engine No. 1095 pulled alongside on an unscheduled stop specially to pick me up. Such is the communication and efficiency of the V.R. who, realising my dilemma, had made arrangements for the northbound train to be specially stopped. After much waving, smiling and shouting between the crews, not a word of which could I understand, I was being whisked northwards again – all within a few seconds!

It was on this journey that I again encountered one of the great truths about steam engines, simply that all of them are individuals. For enthusiasts all engines have an individuality but so do they to engine-men, albeit in a completely different way. When we set off from that remote stop I noticed that 1095's pressure gauge registered some way short of its 213 lbs per sq. in. and despite much work from the fireman throughout our run the engine was, to some extent, steam-shy. This was especially noticeable after my run with 1096 when almost the full pressure had been maintained regardless of working conditions. Upon mentioning this to a V.R. official at Kouvola the following day he said with a gesture 'But of course 1095 is steam-shy; everyone knows that', whereupon he proceeded to tell me what a superb engine 1096 was!

Such experiences inevitably endeared me to the Tr1s and it was wonderful to be amongst them at Kouvola where, on certain days, as many as twelve might be in steam, although the majority would be standby engines in readiness for a sudden upsurge in traffic from the Russian border. Plate 3 depicts Tr1 No. 1093, one of the Whitte smoke-deflector and roller-bearing engines, leaving Kouvola with a freight for Kotka. Despite the fact that work for the class was spas-modic, all Tr1s remained in traffic early in 1972, although quite a few were stored. During my visit to Kuopio Works I saw three receiving overhauls. This is done to provide for a possible motive power shortage for which the V.R. has determined to keep sixty Ristos in running order until 1975.

The class's last principal haunt is Kouvola, from where they work to Pieksämäki, Kotka, Hamina, Vainikkälä, Riihimäki and Helsinki. Their working into Helsinki involves running under overhead electrification and this was forbidden until recently when the V.R. developed an insulation cage which fits over the tender. This device dispenses with any potential danger of a short circuit from the wires and it is so effective that the fireman can even water down the coal without risk, whilst it affords protection should the engine prime. Another important centre for the class is Pieksämäki, from where they work freights to Kouvola, Jyväskylä and Iisalmi.

V.R. Pr1 class 2–8–2T   Plate No. 54

Finland is not a country of big sprawling cities. In fact it is quite the reverse, a place where there seems to be both time and space for everyone and perhaps this is more readily understood when one considers that the population is only 4.6 million. Britain, which has a smaller square mileage (94,220 against Finland's 130,000) has some 55 million! Accordingly Finland has relatively little need for suburban passenger engines. However this small batch of exceedingly fine looking 2–8–2Ts was built for suburban services around Helsinki, the capital, to replace the older Vk1, Vk2 and Vk3 classes of 2–6–4Ts.

Although of Finnish design, the first eight engines were built by Hanomag of Hanover in 1924, who in the same year produced the first of the V.R.'s hump-shunting 0–10–0Ts, classified Vr3. Visibly the two types are remarkably identical, for apart from their boilers and cylinders, the smokebox, saddle tank and cab are all the same. The Vr3s have an axle loading of 15.6 tons compared with Pr1's 15 tons, and it is interesting to note that the 0–10–0T yields a tractive effort at 85 per cent boiler pressure of 37,390 lbs, whilst the 2–8–2T, which in terms of tractive effort calculation is identical in every way except in its driving wheels, produces a figure of 29,700 lbs. Thus the Vr3s, with five axles and 4 ft 2-in.-diameter driving wheels, achieve a lighter power rating than the Pr1s, with four axles and 5 ft 3-in.-wheels. Of course the Pr1s' larger wheels enabled them to work up to sprightly speeds of 55 m.p.h. whilst their cart horse relation was restricted to 30 m.p.h.

150

Production of Pr1s moved to Finland in 1925, when two further engines emerged from Lokomo's Workshops, and the contingent of sixteen was rounded off in 1926 with four more from Lokomo and two from Tampella. Both the Pr1s and the Vr3s were to fulfil adequately their respective working roles over the following fifty years, the Pr1s acquiring the nickname 'Paikku', which means almost the same as 'local train', whilst the Vr3s became known as 'Cocks'.

It is possible that more Pr1s might have been built had not the V.R. obtained four huge 4–6–4Ts from Henschel of Germany as World War II reparations. Originally intended for Estonia, these highly un-Finnish looking engines were also used on the Helsinki suburban traffic, being classified Pr2, but they rolled badly on the light track and after a serious accident, involving a collapsed firebox crownplate, they were withdrawn. Rather remarkably one is scheduled for inclusion in Finland's national railway museum and although it will make a strange and impressive exhibit one cannot help wondering why such an ill-fated and unrepresentative type should be chosen in favour of the Pr1s which, it appears, are scheduled to pass into extinction.

The Pr1s were well known for their rapid acceleration and high speed running, there never being any shortage of power despite their being officially restricted to 55 m.p.h. Until well into the 1960s these Paikkus were a familiar sight at Helsinki's terminal station, but with the advance of dieselisation they became scattered throughout Finland, mainly as shunting engines at more important junctions. In fact for the rest of their days their usage was limited principally to goods yards and short freight trips, because of the class's rather small water capacity of only 3,375 gallons. Such work hardly befitted them and by the early 'seventies only six survived on the V.R.'s stock list and of these, No. 763, the engine illustrated, was the only one in use. Others are on standby at Iisalmi and Joensuu, whilst at Kouvola two rusting survivors lie dumped, one partly dismanted. It was to Kouvola that the first two emigrated from Helsinki in the 1950s.

The plate was made by courtesy of the V.R. authorities in Pieksämäki, who offered to steam up the engine specially in order that a working example could be included in this series – thus giving some compensation to posterity for not preserving one! Early upon the day in question, I was actually awoken by No. 763's whistle as the engine went about her duties around the station yard, having been put on a shunting diagram instead of the usual diesel. Such a gesture is typical of the consideration and thoughtfulness possessed by the Finns and is in accord with their welcoming approach to any foreigner with an interest in their culture.

One interesting feature about No. 763, which incidentally is one of the original Hanomag engines, is that her boiler had never been used on a Vr3 although it had been fitted to three other Pr1s over the years. When the plate was made the engine had in fact retained the same boiler for seven years, but these facts do bear out the traditional allegation that a locomotive's real identity is in its frames and perhaps its cylinders. In April 1972 No. 763 was due for a boiler test, the last overhaul date having been Novemeber 1968, and it was doubted whether the engine would be overhauled again despite a keen awareness at Pieksämäki that she was the last of her kind.

The main dimensions are: cylinders $22\frac{1}{2}$ in. × $25\frac{1}{2}$ in., driving wheel diameter 5 ft 3 in., boiler pressure 171 lbs per sq. in., and grate area $22\frac{3}{4}$ sq. ft. The total length is $43\frac{1}{2}$ ft and weight in working order no less than 88 tons, including a coal carrying capacity of 4 tons.

V.R. Vr1 class 0–6–0T   Rear endpaper

Whilst filming these engines shunting at Kouvola I found a certain familiarity about them that I was unable to explain. Eventually the realisation came to me that they were ideal subjects for modelling, since they epitomised the attractive and solidly-built little shunting engine always to be found gracing model layouts. They would make an ideal blueprint for an internationally acceptable engine to fulfil this purpose. Bearing this in mind I have attempted to do their character full justice by portraying them from a side view.

On a more practical note, the type has other claims to universality having been adopted in 1913 as Finland's standard shunting engine. Prior to the Vr1s' introduction, Finnish shunting locomotives consisted of an assortment of old main line types such as the C1.2.4 and five 0–6–0s, along with some English-built B1 0–4–2STs which dated back to 1868. Over the years, traffic had been increasing continually, so creating the need for a really suitable shunter. Many of these older types were becoming winded and the Vr1s, with their tractive effort of 13,780 lbs at 65 per cent boiler pressure, compared with the 7,275 lbs-odd of the older engines, were destined to fulfil all requirements for many years to come. The type has an axle loading of 15 tons.

Accordingly, 1913 saw the first fifteen ordered from Tampella. At that time they were intended for wood burning and so had large spark-arresting chimneys which looked exciting if slightly odd on so small an engine, although in contrast some later examples were built as coal burners. The initial eleven had straight-topped side tanks, thus markedly distinguishing themselves from all later engines, which had a characteristic forward slope for increased visibility (see illustration). Another difference in the early engines was their construction in saturated form, but they were later rebuilt with superheaters during the mid-1920s. Originally designated L1, they became Vr1 under a reclassification scheme in 1942, but throughout their lives they were more popularly known as 'Hens', a name which, according to a Finnish friend of mine, was bestowed upon them because of their tendency to 'peck' when running. Quite what he meant by this I have been trying to puzzle out ever since! However, the class quickly became very popular with the crews who found them easy to handle and quick to reverse – two fundamental requisites in a shunting engine, as all locomotive men will know. Six Vr1s were captured by the Russians in 1918 during the Finnish War of Liberation although four of these were returned in 1928.

A further ten appeared in 1921 with five from Tampella and five from Hanomag of Germany, this builder producing a further five in 1923, and the engine illustrated is the last of this set – Hanomag No. 10265 of 1923. Note the attractive worksplate. These locomotives were ordered from Germany as a result of the setbacks inflicted upon Finnish industry during the war of independence. Another thirteen came from Tampella in 1925–6, thus bringing the total number built to forty-three. The class was put to work in shunting yards throughout the entire country, giving many years of premium service until the encroachment of diesel shunters in the 1960s.

During their resultant demise, fifteen were acquired by the army and stored away in full working order, whilst the V.R. also adopted a policy of storing rather than scrapping, so much so in fact that some two-thirds of the entire class could still be accounted for in 1972, albeit that a few were dumped in derelict condition. In 1940 two further engines had been lost to Russia, thus bringing the total to four, and the fate of these remains unknown, although two were certainly still working there in 1968 – and what a welcome variety they must have made in this country of highly standardised designs. They came to be the V.R.'s oldest steam engines and among their last retreats were Lahti, Kouvola and Kotka. The design was very much in accordance with Finnish traditions, but one absent feature was the air-operated pedals for opening the firehold doors. Although latterly coal-fired, many still retain their wood-burning chimneys. At the time of writing no VR1s are set by for preservation but a superb scaled-down model of one may be seen at Helsinki Railway Museum. The illustration depicts a Vr1 standing in front of a house which once belonged to an important railway official.

The Vr1s' leading data are: cylinders 17 in. × 21¾ in., boiler pressure 171 lbs per sq. in., driving wheel diameter 4 ft 2 in. and grate area 16 sq. ft. Fuel capacities are 2 tons of coal and 788 gallons of water, whilst the engine's total weight in full working order is 45 tons, contained in a length of 31 ft.

V.R. Vr2 class 0–6–2T   Front endpaper

By 1927 the final examples of Finland's standard class of shunters, the Vr1 0–6–0Ts (see rear endpaper) had been built. Traffic was continually increasing, so bringing the need for more powerful engines, but axle weight restrictions remained a continually limiting factor. Accordingly, a modified range of shunting locomotives was built having the same diameter driving wheels but with the 0–6–2 wheel arrangement, the trailing axle allowing an appreciably more powerful locomotive to operate on an axle load of only 14.8 tons, as compared with the Vr1's 15 tons. Originally classified 01, and later Vr2, the new engines were altogether more powerful-looking machines and were nearly 4 ft longer than their forerunners and 13 tons heavier. A total of sixteen was built, all coming from Tampella between 1930 and 1931. It was also intended that these engines should be capable of some main line tripping work and accordingly their coal and water capacities were 2½ tons and 1,208 gallons.

Despite the class's being superficially similar in appearance to the Vr1s, the cylinders and boilers of the two types differed, the Vr2s having cylinders of 17¾ in. × 23½ in. compared with the Vr1's 17 in. × 21¾ in., whilst the Vr2's total heating surface was some 150 sq. ft greater. The differences culminated in a tractive effort of 21,500 lbs for the Vr2, some 3,500 lbs higher than the Vr1's, at 85 per cent of boiler pressure, which in both designs was 171 lbs per sq. in. It is interesting to note that this difference in power was achieved over an extra 1.2 sq. ft of grate area.

The Ducks, as the Vr2 became known, never possessed quite the agility that the Vr1s were so noted for and perhaps this is one of the reasons why they remained at only sixteen engines. It was intended to build more after World War II, but because of industrial pressures the builders could not cope with the order and the engines were destined never to be built. This cancelling of the order was possibly due to the V.R.'s obtaining twenty-four Vr4 Vulcan 0–6–0STs on a special transaction of surplus American locomotives. However, it is doubtful if much was gained from this as they had to be converted to 0–6–2STs by the V.R. to reduce the axle weight, which even in rebuilt form was 17.3 tons. Reclassified Vr5, these Turkeys were the only alien type to survive on Finnish metals in the 1970s.

The illustration depicts a particularly interesting aspect of Finnish locomotives in the orange-coloured acetylene gas cylinder situated on the running plate. This was the original form of lighting and although many later engines had turbo generators for electricity, quite a number were still using acetylene gas at the time of my visit, including some Vr1s (see endpaper) and Tk3s. In their latter days all Vr2s burned coal, but only one engine lost its ballon-stacked chimney. Many people are suprised that Finland should revert from wood burning, especially in view of their dense woodlands, but apart from national economics, the locomotives' availability was an important factor. The wood burners needed bunkering up much more often than their coal burning counterparts, owing to wood having greater bulk for the same calorific value.

During the early 1950s, modifications were made to the Vr2s' cabsides, which were swelled outwards for improved visibility, and this tended to give the engines an even more modern appearance. Apart from three engines stored by the Army, all remained on the V.R.'s active list in 1972, and I was treated to the sight of one in resplendently overhauled condition on running-in tests between Kuopio Works and Pieksämäki. Nevertheless many were spare to diesels and their final stamping grounds were the heavy marshalling yards at Haapamäki, Jyväskylä, Joensuu, Toijala and Seinäjoki. All sixteen are destined for eventual storage by the Army, none being retained for preservation.

The picture was made after I had received a message from Jyväskylä saying that a Vr2 was scheduled to deputise for a failed diesel that night. I was staying at Pieksämäki at the time and so it was that I journeyed over by train to film V.R. No. 961, Tampella No. 450 of 1931. Dusk fell as the railcar mused its way over the attractive 53-mile journey and through the gathering gloom I was afforded a fleeting glimpse of stored engines. The forlorn silhouettes of these engines stowed away deep in the woods made an eerie sight. Upon arrival at Jyväskylä I was greeted by the spectacle and sounds of No. 961

intrepidly engaged in fly shunting, buffeting and rolling wagons in all directions. Some of the loads she was moving were quite vast but the blades in the spark-arresting chimney muffled her exhaust to little more than a gentle sigh, although the engine rather compensated for this by continually oozing out steam in all directions, a characteristic which I was anxious to capture for the picture.

FRANCE

S.N.C.F. 141R class 2–8–2   Plate Nos. 2, 44, 45

The morning air smelled both pure and sweet as I carefully made my way through the thickets of tomato and peach groves which grew alongside the River Algy at Rivesaltes, a small town on the French south coast. It was barely 6.00 a.m. on a cloudless July morning but already the Mediterranean sun was beginning to make its presence felt, and descending a steep bank past an orchard of apricot trees, whose crop had already been harvested a few weeks previously, I found myself in the bed of a dried-up tributary of the Algy. The tranquillity was broken only by the sounds of birds engaged in breeding activities. Climbing up from the tributary's stony bed and traversing further groves I arrived at my destination, a spot beside the Algy itself commanding a view of the stone viaduct carrying the S.N.C.F. main line from Narbonne to Spain. With camera at the ready I sat and waited, enjoying the still warmth of this peaceful place and allowing myself to relax a little after the 1,000-mile drive to Rivesaltes. My purpose in visiting this spot was to film the very last of French steam engines, the famous 141R 2–8–2s which, after a rapid demise during the late 'sixties and early 'seventies, were ending their days working between Narbonne and the Spanish border. Some fifteen 141Rs survived on these duties, the end of 145 years of steam traction on French Railways. As is well known, the 141Rs went to France as liberation engines after the ravages of World War II and were supplied by America after a desperate appeal for help by the French authorities. Whilst I filmed the 141Rs at Rivesaltes their history was to the forefront of my mind and I was struck by the contrast between the circumstances of their birth in war-torn Europe and the peaceful surroundings of their duties along the Mediterranean coast of France. Poignancy was added to the occasion by an old French landworker who stopped to pass the time of day. His wrinkled face burnished by innumerable summers bore more than a hint of past tragedy and he readily expressed his awareness of the origins of the 'liberation machines' which still ran through his home town, proceeding to tell me of his years spent as a prisoner of war under the Nazis. A little after 7.30 a.m. the rhythms of an approaching freight became audible and excitement mounted as a 141R rumbled over the viaduct emitting a glorious exhaust trail. The engine was hauling a northbound freight from Spain and plate 45 depicts this scene.

My pictures at Rivesaltes and Narbonne depict the end of these celebrated engines, but to see them in perspective we must go back to the latter days of World War II when, as a result of sabotage and air attacks by the allies on German-occupied France, the country's total of 17,000 locomotives in service was reduced to 3,000 by the time of the German evacuation, many of these being badly run down by the turmoil of four years of Nazi occupation. Furthermore, a vast amount of railway installations – and indeed industry in general – was rendered useless, with the result that a state of emergency existed. When the allies invaded France, many British and American engines were sent to supplement the meagre French stock, including the M.O.S. Riddles Austerity 2-8-0/2-10-0s and the American Transportation Corps 2-8-0s. Although a rapid repair programme was carried out, recovery of the French resources was inevitably going to take some years, and from a motive power viewpoint extra problems were created by the difficulty experienced in recovering the many S.N.C.F. engines taken away by the Germans for use elsewhere.

The French appealed to America, giving details of the kind of locomotive needed, and this led to the French Railway Mission's visiting America to discuss the new engines with the Baldwin Loco-motive Works in Philadelphia. It was agreed that Baldwins should design the new engines for simultaneous production by themselves, Lima of Ohio and the American Locomotive Company (Alco) of Schenectady. In order to facilitate a quick delivery, the Americans stated that whilst the new engines would not be Austerity, they must fit in with American design practice although the basic French require-ment for a 2-8-2 would be adhered to, as well as the basic demand that the engines must be simple, robust, mixed-traffic machines capable of turning a hand to anything demanded of them. Accordingly the 141Rs, as the new engines became known, were steeped in Ameri-can traditions and in fact were a direct descendent from a World War I utility 2-8-2 – a type built as a war-time standard for American railways. By March 1945 work had begun and by the beginning of 1946 – just a little over a year after the French Mission had visited Baldwins to finalise the plans – no less than 700 engines had been built.

In July 1945 the first 141R, named *Liberation,* was steamed at Lima's Works amid a special ceremony during which the engine ran through a large paper barrier in French national colours. The name *Liberation* was to become applied to the class as a whole over its earlier years, but latterly they have simply been known by the French as *L'Americaines.* When the first batch arrived at Marseilles in November 1945 they were greeted by yet another ceremony, and so commenced the work of these brilliant engines upon French soil.

After the initial batch of 700, orders were given for a further 640, 500 from the three American companies previously stated, and the remaining 140 from two Canadian builders, the Montreal Locomotive Company and the Canadian Locomotive Company. By 1947 the entire consignment of 1,323 engines (of the Montreal Locomotive Co's engines 17 were lost at sea en route to France) had been delivered. It is interesting to note the confidence the French placed in this design, as the first batch of 700 had virtually been completed before the first example had run trials on French soil. The actual building quantities for each workshop were Lima 280, Alco 460, Baldwin 460, Montreal Locomotive Company 100 and the Canadian Locomotive Company 40.

Although they looked superficially alike, various differences occurred within the 141Rs' ranks. The first 700, which had plain bearings and spoked driving wheels, were traditional coal burners and remained so throughout their working lives, but 300 of the second batch were constructed as oil burners whilst a further 320 were converted to oil-burning in France. Earlier engines of the second batch had roller bearings and Boxpok wheels on their driving axle, whereas the final 240 built had roller bearings and Boxpok driving wheels on all axles. Typical American features were provided such as steam-powered reversing gear, in addition to mechanical stokers on the coal-burning engines, but the American aura was considerably offset by the distinctively French windshields and oblong buffers. The class's impressive eight-wheeled tenders were mounted on two bogies. When delivered, all 141Rs were black, but over the years many acquired a green livery with various styles of lining-out, and their decking out in sparkling green did much to heighten their rugged attractiveness.

Upon spreading to most parts of the S.N.C.F. network, the 141Rs quickly proved themselves well capable of hauling 800-ton trains on level track at 65 m.p.h., and accordingly they formed an effective backbone for French steam power over the remainder of its existence. Truly mixed-traffic engines in every way, their duties ranged from heavy main line express work on tight schedules to meandering cross-country freight trains, and although they were rather rough engines to ride on, their complete reliability and remarkably free steaming capacities greatly endeared them to the French enginemen. So despite the 141Rs' originally being intended as a stud of hastily-produced stop-gap engines designed to cover dire emergencies, they became engines of long term importance and as late as 1970 – twenty-five years after their inception – 141Rs were frequently seen heading the Golden Arrow Express between Calais and Amiens. This success on express passenger trains is partly due to the thrashing they will take, for wide-open regulator and 30 per cent cut-off was a standard method of operation. Their ample boilers never seemed to flag in producing steam and one of the most magnificent sights towards the end of European steam was to see and hear a 141R roaring away at the head of a 1,000-ton train.

Their leading dimensions are as follows: 2 cylinders $23\frac{1}{2}$ in. × 28 in., driving wheel diameter 5 ft 5 in., boiler pressure 220 lbs per sq. in., grate area $55\frac{1}{2}$ sq. ft and tractive effort at 85 per cent boiler pressure 44,500 lbs. Their boilers gave them a total evaporative surface of 2,699 sq. ft, including a superheater surface of 704 sq. ft. The total weight of the engine was 112 tons and its axle loading 19.7 tons.

So, with this sparkling fusion of American and French design, the steam locomotive came to an end in France and, of the 15,000 engines held by the French during the early fifties, only a handful of 141Rs remain on the Mediterranean coast. At the time of writing, it is expected that these engines will finish about the end of 1972. Throughout steam's rundown in France it was common to see rusting 141Rs dumped in weed-covered sidings, whilst the hulks of others could be seen partly cut up on depot scrap lines – making a weird contrast with the many examples still engaged upon important duties. Over the last year of their existence 141Rs were for sale at scrap prices of £950, whilst many were scheduled to go to the Fiat Works in Milan as material for new cars – a sign of the times indeed! However, quite a number have been retained and stored in full working order in case another crisis should call for a 141R.

In a country like France, eventual preservation seems a foregone conclusion and with the arrival in Britain of an S.N.C.F. 231G Pacific and an ex-Nord 230D 4-6-0, perhaps one day a 141R might be found amongst the ever-growing number of foreign engines preserved in Britain. At any rate it makes an interesting speculation.

ITALY

The small selection of Italian steam engines featured in this volume provides an introduction to the diverse and impressive array of locomotives at work in Italy during the 1970s. It is remarkable that a country with so high a standard of living should retain something like 1,000 steam locomotives – the current figure on the F.S. books – and, furthermore, that they should range over some fifteen different types. Even more remarkable is their average age of 50-60 years, for all steam design and building finished in Italy as long ago as the 1920s. Unlike its neighbour Yugoslavia, Italy has now shed all Austrian, German, Prussian, American and British types that worked on its territory as a result of two world wars, and the majority of the present locomotives on the F.S. are standard designs which, either directly or indirectly, can be traced back to the Italian motive power standardisation scheme implemented as far back as 1905. In that year the F.S. (Italian State Railways), was formed from the amalgamation of three principal concerns, the Mediterranean System (R.M.), the Adriatic System (R.A.), and the Sicilian System (R.S.). Guiseppi Zara, former mechanical engineer of the Adriatic System, became responsible for locomotive development on the F.S. and he wasted no time whatsoever in devising a range of twelve standard types intended to cover all Italy's requirements, so making her one of the first countries in Europe to implement such a well-integrated scheme.

The principal requirement for these standards was lightness in construction with low axle loadings, because Italian track mileage at that time consisted of very light rail weighing only 73 lbs per yard. Another vital factor was economy in fuel consumption in view of Italy's lack of natural coal resources and her reliance upon costly imported fuel. Zara chose saturated compounds for his standards and began to construct a range of engines in which the 2-6-0, 2-6-2 and 2-8-0 wheel arrangements predominated, along with sets of 2-6-0 and 0-6-0 tank engines. The advent of superheating in Italy a few years later rather upset the scheme but nevertheless, despite a number of modifications and departures from the original designs, evidence of the 1905 scheme predominates in the country today.

It has frequently been stated that twentieth-century Italian locomotives were never dynamic performers and whilst this is undoubtedly true, the Italian's highly individualistic school of engines has served all essential needs. One of their principal deficiencies was their rigid adherence to short-travel valves, whilst restricted steam passages to and from the valves constituted an indifferent front-end design. Aesthetically, F.S. locomotives are well characterised by their quaint spring-balance safety valves, stovepipe chimneys, coned smokebox doors, round-topped fireboxes and non-side-window cabs. Whatever the shortcomings of their locomotives, Italian engineers have contributed some dramatic innovations to the traditional steam engine, such as the Zara Truck, Caprotti Valve Gear and Franco-Crosti boilers – all developments which not only contributed to the uniqueness of Italian steam engines but which, in one form or another, spread to many parts of the world during the latter days of steam locomotive development.

Italy's remarkably early cessation of steam design in the 1920s is partly understandable in a land reliant upon imported coal yet possessing abundant water supplies for electricity. Main line electrification began in 1914, and today Italy sports some vintage electric locomotives which act as an interesting foil to their ever-ageing steam fleet. Actually, electrification was begun in Italy as early as 1902, with two routes radiating from the northern town of Lecco, and yet over seventy years later a few steam engines can still be seen in that town.

Over many years now the F.S. has restricted its steam fleet to secondary lines, so that the greater concentration of steam can be found in the more populated northern areas although, contrary to the practice of many countries, steam is maintained throughout much of Italy and is used, often 'under the wires', on local freight and ballast duties. Consequently, Italy has very few of the 'steam free' areas which many other countries proudly announce. Some time ago the F.S. emphatically declared their intention to abolish steam by 1972, but this was destined not to happen and it is possible that a few of the antiquities from their delightful and fiercely individualistic locomotive family will still be apparent as the 1980s approach. A further selection of F.S. locomotives will appear in a later volume of this series.

Preservation is reasonably well covered by museum representation in Italy, but as yet no enthusiast-backed working lines have emerged, as they have in most other western countries, though there is still sufficient time for this to occur.

F.S. 625 class 2–6–0 Plate No. 46

Nationalisation of Italian railways occurred in 1905 and amongst the range of twelve standard designs subsequently produced by Guiseppi Zara were two classes of medium-sized saturated two-cylinder compound 2–6–0. These were the 600 class for mixed traffic duties and the 630 class for passenger work, appearing in 1905 and 1906 respectively. Intended for use throughout the F.S. system, both types had standard boilers and inside cylinders with outside Walschaerts valve gear, and were almost identical in appearance except that the 630s had immense 6 ft 1-in.-diameter driving wheels, compared with the 600 class's 5 ft 0-in. ones. Italy's standardisation plan was largely based on non-superheated compounds and the advent of superheating some years later upset the scheme by causing a shift in policy towards simple expansion. Accordingly, in 1907 the two-cylinder simple superheated 640 class was introduced, followed three years later by the two-cylinder simple superheated 625 class, these two classes being the improved 630 and 600 classes respectively. This meant, of course, that two standard classes were running in two different forms, although all further building was to the simple-superheated pattern. The 625s were built up to 1923, whilst construction of the 640s did not cease until 1930, by which time 173 had been completed. Building was undertaken in Italy, Austria and Germany. Some engines from the original 600/630 classes were rebuilt to conform with their 625/640 counterparts during the mid 'twenties and early 'thirties, a process which involved a reduction of boiler pressure from the original 229 lbs per sq. in. to 171 lbs per sq. in.

Whilst this rebuilding was taking place the opportunity was taken to incorporate Caprotti valve gear in place of the original Walschaerts, and altogether 156 rebuilt 600s and 16 rebuilt 630s were so treated, thus becoming the first locomotives extensively to use this Italian-designed valve gear which had first been tried out on a 740 class 2–8–0 in 1921. The Caprotti system, which was the idea of an Italian motor engineer, greatly improved the steam distribution by using vertical poppet valves operated from rotating cams, and was an immense

162

improvement on the short-travel valves used on most other F.S. locomotives. The idea was taken up in many countries, along with the similar Austrian Lentz gear system, although the advantages became lessened once long-travel valves became regularly applied. However, it is an interesting point that Caprotti Valve Gear was used on B.R.'s *Duke of Gloucester* which attained the lowest steam consumption per h.p.-hour of any simple expansion locomotive known. Altogether some 400 Italian engines received Caprotti Valve Gear, but over more recent years when maintenance of the ever-declining steam fleet has become more specialised, they have been phased out and today all surviving engines use Walschaerts gear with short-travel valves.

After finally consolidating the 600/625s into one basically standard form the F.S. created a further divergence within the class's ranks by fitting thirty-five engines with Franco-Crosti boilers (see page 166) in 1952-3 (and classifying them 623). Of this thirty-five some were ex-600 rebuilds, so the 623s that resulted possessed both Walschaerts and Caprotti Valve Gear engines. One of the principal duties of the 623 class was operating trains between Venice and Bassano – see plate 46, although when this picture was made in 1971 all 623s were out of traffic owing to their being non-standard types, and the last few survivors were stored at Rimini.

It was upon the inception of the 600 class in 1905 that Guiseppi Zara introduced his famous 'Zara Truck' or 'Italian Bogie' whereby the leading axle and first set of driving wheels were mounted together in a bogie frame and the driving axle, although set in main frame axle boxes, was arranged to slide laterally. The F.S.'s sharply curved secondary lines could be negotiated at high speeds using this arrangement and the Italian Bogie was so successful that it became a standard fitting on all F.S. locomotives possessing a leading pair of wheels, except the 735 class 2-8-0s (see page 165). To compensate for the side movement in the driving axles, ball-shaped coupling rod journals are used with specially-shaped brasses, although the trucks pivot in such a way as to allow most side play in the radial wheels and less in the leading coupled wheels. This device is similar in principal to the better-known Krauss Truck.

Purely Italian in every possible way, the 625/640s possess another Zara speciality whereby their inside cylinders are operated by outside valve gear and steam chests. In providing inside cylinders, Zara was able to use the lightest possible plate frames so as to keep a low axle loading for Italy's secondary routes. Positioning the valve gear outside gave better access for maintenance, whilst lack of eccentrics in the crank axle gave more room for adequate bearing surfaces. This arrangement strongly characterises these classes and upon encountering it for the first time one gets a weird sensation of seeing an engine driven only by its steam chests. This effect is at its greatest when one watches the 640s at speed with their huge wheels a whisking tapestry of Walschaerts motion and no cylinders! Another flair point in the class's character is the separate rectangular sandboxes mounted ahead of the steam dome, for in later Italian practice both were incorporated into one housing.

The 625s have $19\frac{1}{4} \times 27$-in. cylinders, driving wheels of 5 ft 0 in. diameter, a boiler pressure of 171 lbs per sq. in. and a grate area of 26 sq. ft, whilst the total weight in full working order is 56 tons. The 640s by contrast have an extra 2 in. cylinder diameter and of course 6 ft 1-in. driving wheels. Both classes have Italy's standard 2,640-gallon tenders.

I regard the 625s as one of Europe's most interesting classes, for apart from their gaunt vintage delineation, they are perfect representatives of the Italian school. Many still survive, especially in northern Italy, at Verona, Cremona and Venice, whilst a few still work in Sicily. No 625s are scheduled for preservation although a 640 is stored in Rome awaiting restoration and it is likely that the Italians will regard this engine as sufficiently representative of the two classes.

My most poignant memory of the 625s was created one evening at Piádena, a remote junction in northern Italy where the Parma–Bréscia and Cremona–Mantova routes cross. It was during the summer of 1972 and four 625-hauled passenger trains were scheduled to be in the station simultaneously. Angry storm clouds dominated the blue dusk as one by one the 625s arrived hauling short rakes of ancient coaching stock, and the quality of the evening light gave the scene a luminosity making it not unlike a Victorian Print. The four engines stood in Piádena's modern station like ghosts from an era long since gone, their darkened archaic forms issuing palls of smoke into the evening air, so creating a rare confrontation with the modern colour signals. After a few minutes the trains departed one after another, with their whistles wailing across the still countryside and their smoke trails echoing the sky's cloudy burden. Rain began to fall as the last train pulled out amid haloes of steam. Silently I watched its wobbling tail light disappear into the gloom, sensing as I did so the atmosphere of loneliness which crept over Piádena.

The 740 class was introduced as a standard superheated two-cylinder simple freight engine in 1911, and over the following twelve years a total of 470 was constructed. Apart from being Italy's most numerous class, the 740s were destined to serve the F.S. over the ensuing sixty years and even today they abound in considerable numbers. Construction was undertaken principally in Italy, although some engines came from Henschel of Germany. In common with the 625 class (see page 162) they owe their origin to an earlier set of two-cylinder compound engines and the 740s were a development of Guiseppi Zara's non-superheated 730 class 2-8-0s, produced under the F.S. standardisation programme in 1905.

No sooner was construction well under way than World War I broke out, leaving the F.S. without enough 740s to cope with wartime needs. Accordingly, in 1916 the Italians approached America for locomotives and handed over the 740 drawings to Alco, requesting an urgent delivery of identical engines. Alco obliged and supplied 393 engines between 1917 and 1919. Although the basic 740 dimensions were incorporated, the new engines differed in having such improvements over the basic design as bar frames, tapered boilers and long-travel valves, and thus were considerably superior to the pure Italian engines. Classified 735, the American engines were the only F.S. designed locomotives possessing leading wheels not fitted with a Zara Truck. With a combined total of 863 engines, the 735/740 classes were the backbone of Italy's heavy freight power. But despite the 735s' superiority, very few now remain in service, although forty have been sold to Greece.

In 1921 another variation appeared on the basic 740 design in the shape of the 940 class 2-8-2 tank engines with identical boiler, cylinders and wheels. Fifty-three examples of these impressive machines were built between 1921 and 1924 and in common with the 740s quite a number are still active, being employed on steeply-graded lines for freight and banking work, whilst one is already preserved in the Museum of Science and Technology, Milan. 1921 is also of interest in discussing the 740s' history, for during that year one of the class was fitted with Caprotti Valve Gear (see page 162), so becoming the first locomotive in the world to receive this Italian innovation. Five sister engines were subsequently fitted, although none remain in traffic today as this development is now regarded as non-standard.

Quite apart from the 740s' distinction as Italy's twentieth-century freight engines, they have achieved wider fame, with far reaching implications, as a result of the class's being used so extensively in the Franco and Franco-Crosti boiler experiments. This fascinating Italian masterpiece was a gallant attempt at utilising the hot gasses more fully. The tube elements were altered to release hot gasses into the smokebox at a higher temperature than usual. Then, by feeding them back through two large pre-heater drums containing the boiler feed water, the gasses were exhausted at the locomotive's firebox end at a much lower temperature than on conventional steam engines, thus utilising their maximum heat-giving potential. By this method the feed water was brought up to boiler pressure in the pre-heater drums and was then fed into the boiler through a clack valve. Quite apart from the extra utilisation of heat, this system possesses some practical advantages in that any scale deposits from the water settle in the pre-heater instead of in the engine's boiler, whilst another maintenance-saving advantage is the avoidance of harmful effects created by water being injected at low temperature into a fully-steaming boiler, as in most normal locomotives. Five 740 locomotives were so converted in 1941 and an estimated 10 per cent saving in coal consumption led to a further eighty-nine engines' being converted up to 1953. These modified engines, which have a pre-heater and chimney on either side of the boiler, are known as Franco-Crosti engines, and were re-classified 743. Such a saving in coal consumption was admirable, especially in a country reliant upon imported coal. It has been suggested that Britain's sanctions against Italy in 1936 precipitated the Franco-Crosti experiments, for up until that time Italy had been largely dependent upon British coal.

In 1955, a further development occurred within this context when a 740 was rebuilt with a single pre-heater unit slung underneath the main boiler. This arrangement, known as the Crosti boiler, was in principal identical with the earlier rebuilds except that the pre-heater was largely concealed and only one chimney was necessary, which was situated on the fireman's side. The engine was reclassified 741 and a further eighty were constructed in 1959–60 so bringing the total of 740s converted to either the Franco-Crosti or the Crosti boiler to 175. Throughout all these conversions the original 740 boiler was retained, the pre-heaters simply being added to it. The lack of a conventionally-placed chimney gave both variations a beheaded appearance, but the discreet placing of the pre-heater drum on the 741s made more gainly-looking engines, although they lacked the 743s' deliciously grotesque ironmongery. One can hardly imagine more unusual-looking engines than the 743s, but when some of them were streamlined their appearance became truly incredible and in view of their sheer uniqueness it is a tragedy that none survive in this form today. I often wonder how the opponents of Bullied's air-smoothed Pacifics would have reacted to a streamlined Franco-Crosti!

There were, however, some problems with these seemingly efficient systems, the greatest being metal corrosion in the pre-heater tubes and chimney. This was caused by the low-temperature exhaust gasses releasing sulphuric acid. On traditional steam engines the exhaust gasses usually leave the chimney at about 350°C., compared with about 200°C. on a Crosti. With average coals, sulphuric acid condenses out at around 275°C., too low a temperature to concern a traditional steam engine, but one which rendered the Crosti highly vulnerable. The problem can be minimised by using coal of very low sulphur content, assuming of course that consistent supplies of such coal can be obtained efficiently, but more effective has been the use of chrome steel for certain affected parts, although it is still quite commonplace to see jagged chimney tops on 741/3s showing where the metal has been eaten away. Another difficulty encountered has been indifferent steaming as the long passages impair the exhaust blast, whilst furthermore this weakened exhaust can lead to smoke drifting into the cab, so making these engines dirty to work upon. Nevertheless, it is surprising that so few countries have experimented with these boilers, especially over the latter days of steam development, and in fact only a few engines in Germany, Belgium, Spain and Britain were ever converted. Nowhere were the innovations so numerous as in Italy, where some 215 locomotives have been adapted (see also page 163), and now Italy remains the only country in the world to retain this fascinating system, with quite large numbers of class 741/3 still in operation.

The class's leading dimensions are: 2 cylinders $21\frac{1}{4}$ in. × $27\frac{1}{2}$ in., boiler pressure 171 lbs per sq. in., driving wheel diameter 4 ft $5\frac{1}{2}$ in. and grate area 26.9 sq. ft. Their remarkably light axle loading of 13.4 tons was well within the $16\frac{1}{2}$-ton limit imposed on all Italian steam locomotives, excepting certain Pacifics. Consequently the class has always enjoyed a wide route availability. Total weight of the engine in full working order is 65 tons, although the 741/3 variants are slightly heavier.

Today 740s may be seen at work throughout much of northern Italy, and also on the Italian islands of Sicily and Sardinia, whilst Franco-Crostis still work quite extensively from Alessandria and Cremona. The 741s' most famous duties are operation of traffic on the line through the Dolomite Mountains from Fortezza, on Italy's Austrian border, to San Candido. This line, which is one of the most scenic in Italy, bears fine testimony to these engines – relics from the last attempts to improve the conventional steam locomotive.

I express concern that as yet no Franco-Crosti- or Crosti-boilered engine is scheduled for preservation in Italy. No other countries involved in this experiment retained any of theirs. Consequently we must now look to the innovators themselves to ensure that one of these historically important locomotives is preserved. In this age of both enlightenment and ample resources, it would be totally inexcusable to allow such machines to pass into oblivion, and preservationists would do well to turn their attentions to these remnants of steam's evolution, rather than devoting them to examples of more ordinary engines currently in vogue.

E.A. 0–6–0WT Savona Docks   Plate No. 52

Industrial steam engines still abound in most countries throughout the world, but one could hardly find a more suitable place in which to film and enjoy them than Savona Docks, on the Ligurian Coast of Italy. Savona is one of Italy's biggest ports and although plagued by the inevitable modern hustle, its effect is tempered by the historical styling and elegance of the town. Blessed with a perfect climate throughout the year, Savona's rich golden sands and Mediterranean blue seas are treasures enough, but add to these the varied and fascinating array of ancient steam engines which operate the docks and it becomes a place for the connoisseur indeed. When seen against the background of dockside buildings and quays these locomotives engender reminiscenses of some nineteenth century scene.

This stud of some fourteen engines is owned by Emilio Astengo Soc., a company operating the shunting contract for the docks, and apart from the engine illustrated they own such gems as ex-Italian Sud-Est Railway 0–8–0Ts and ex-F.S. 830/835 class 0–6–0Ts. The 830s were shunting engines on the Mediterranean Railway and forerunners to the better-known 835s – standard shunting engines of the F.S. Two of Emilio Astengo's most distinctive engines are represented by this Henschel 0–6–0 well tank of 1907, E.A. No. 12. This is one of two such engines operating at Savona, the other being numbered E.A. 11 – Henschel works Nos. 8584/5 respectively.

In common with all E.A. engines these two well tanks were obtained second-hand and came from the Grignasco & Coggiola Railway in the Italian province of Vercelli. Both were delivered new to this nine-mile railway when it opened in 1908. The G.C. closed in 1935 and both engines came to Savona Docks. The picture constitutes an evocative study of dockland, the well tank making poignant contrast with a diesel locomotive against a backdrop of wharfside cranes and cargo. In fact only two diesels work at Savona and these were purchased new by E.A. in 1959 and 1964. All other duties are undertaken by steam, though one hears of continual threats to dieselise fully in the near future. Meanwhile amongst the bustling activities of this Ligurian port, a splendid little pocket of steam lives on.

AUSTRIA

O.B.B. 97 class 0–6–2T   Plate No. 17

Details of the history and locomotives of this rack/adhesion line were given in *Twilight of Steam,* page 112, and little more needs to be added here except to say that at the time of this volume's publication, these 1890 0–6–2Ts still reign supreme on many services. The line has become a mecca for enthusiasts from all over the world, indicated by the fact that one of the drivers on the Iron Mountain line offers accommodation to enthusiasts via the columns of leading railway journals. Without doubt this is one of the most interesting and exciting steam-operated lines in Europe.

GERMANY

D.B. 044 class 2–10–0   Plate No. 5

The history of this class was more fully discussed in *Twilight of Steam,* but in view of the inclusion of the ex-Prussian G12 2–10–0s in this volume (see plate No. 11, page 191), some further notes upon the subject might be of interest. The union of Germany's eight state railways in 1920 brought into being the Deutsche Reichsbahn (D.R.B.) and well over 200 different kinds of steam locomotive were inherited by the new administration. The Prussian State Railways were by far the largest constituent, operating over some four-fifths of German territory, and apart from their locomotives' being generally more advanced than those of other states, the Prussians had a huge fleet of standardised types such as the famous P8 4–6–0s (*Twilight of Steam,* page 124), the G8 0–8–0s, of which some 5,000 were built, and the G12 2–10–0s. Thus it followed that upon commencement of the D.R.B. standardisation programme it was Prussian influence which predominated.

The three-cylinder G12s were the first important 2–10–0s to be introduced in Germany and also one of the first of Germany's standard locomotives, as prior to unification they had been built for Prussia, Saxony, Baden and Wurtemberg. They first appeared in 1917, during the latter days of World War I, and building continued up to 1924, by which time little short of 1,500 were at work throughout Germany. Two years later, the three-cylinder 44 class 2–10–0 appeared under the D.R.B.'s standardisation programme and although building proceeded slowly owing to trade recessions, from the mid-'thirties onwards 44s were built in large numbers. The class proved to be immensely important in moving heavy loads during Germany's effort in World War II, exactly as the G12s had been during World War I, and by 1945 1,750 had been constructed. Today the 44s, which have an axle loading of $19\frac{1}{2}$ tons and tractive effort of 60,360 lbs, are one of the most powerful steam engines in Europe. The surviving engines are divided between East and West Germany.

It is interesting to compare the leading dimensions of these two famous 2–10–0 classes.

	Ex-Prussian G12 (later D.R.B. 58 Class)	*D.R.B. 44 Class (later D.B. 044 Class)*
3 cylinders	$22\frac{1}{2}$ in. × 26 in.	$21\frac{3}{8}$ in. × 26 in.
Driving wheel diameter	4 ft $7\frac{1}{8}$ in.	4 ft $7\frac{1}{8}$ in.
Boiler pressure	199 lbs per sq. in.	227 lbs per sq. in.
Grate area	42 sq. ft	49 sq. ft
Axle loading	15.7 tons	$19\frac{1}{2}$ tons

YUGOSLAVIA

To many people, Yugoslavia is a land for idyllic holidays laced with both sunshine and the exquisite beauty of the Adriatic coastline. To others, it is the most westernised communist country, which adheres to non-capitalist philosophies but has no small appetite for the west's standard of living. But for the locomotive enthusiast, Yugoslavia is one of those rare countries which, thanks to its traumatic history, is blessed with as fine an assortment of multi-origined steam engines as one could wish for. Baited by such delights, and in spite of the traditional communist hostility, I determined to feature the country early in this series, before modernisation swept these straggling veterans into history.

We must look into European history to discover why such a range of power should come to Yugoslavia. The country is a federation of six republics: Serbia, Bosnia-Hercegovina, Montenegro, Macedonia, Croatia and Slovenia. These were completely united after the end of World War I under the 'Kingdom of Serbs, Croats and Slovenes' which, in 1929, assumed the title 'Kingdom of Yugoslavia'. The declared basis for this union was ethnic, the desire being to group together all Southern Slavs. The formation of the Kingdom was the result of a union between Serbia and Montenegro and the south-eastern part of the Austro-Hungarian Empire, which included Slovenia, Croatia and Bosnia, Macedonia having previously united with Serbia in 1912. Understandably such a fusion gave the Kingdom a wide diversity of locomotives, the well developed standard gauges of Austria and Hungary predominating in Slovenia and Croatia, whilst Serbia, in totally different traditions, possessed both standard and 760 mm gauges. Although latterly part of the Austrian Empire, Bosnia had developed its own separate network of 760 mm gauge lines. The newly-formed Kingdom continued to order Serbian, Austrian, Bosnian and Hungarian locomotive types, distribution closely following their former geographical territories, until in 1930 the J.D.Z., as the State railways were then known, produced its own indigenous range of standards, so creating further diversity. This period between the wars saw much strengthening of main lines and track doubling, whilst a new main line was created when the 760-mm systems of Croatia and Bosnia were joined up in 1925, so linking Belgrade with Sarajevo.

In 1941 the Yugoslav government allied with Germany against the nation's will and an uprising overthrew the government, whereupon Germany invaded Yugoslavia and divided the country up. Croatia and Bosnia-Hercegovina were grouped into a new Croatian State, Serbia came under German rule and Slovenia was split up between Germany and Italy. An influx of Prussian and German locomotives came as a result of the war, whilst the subsequent reparations made to the

171

re-united Yugoslavia after the cessation of hostilities included engines from Germany, Hungary and Italy. Furthermore many British and American aid engines were sent to help build the country up as 60 per cent of Yugoslav railways had been destroyed.

Throughout the war Yugoslavia's communist party had organised resistance against the occupants and these partisans actually made considerable progress in freeing certain areas. When the war ended it was decided that King Peter would not be reinstated and that General Tito, head of the partisans, would be made President under a constitution which provided that all South Slav nations would have equal rights. President Tito still remains head of Yugoslavia today, the country being known as the Federated Socialist Republic of Yugoslavia.

Since 1933, the J.Z. has adopted the following classificiation schedule for its steam locomotives:

Class numbers are:

01 – 14	Passenger locomotives with tender
15 – 19	Tank engines for main line service
20 – 49	Freight locomotives with tender
50 – 59	Tank engines for freight and local trains
60 – 69	Locomotives for shunting duties
70 – 94	760-mm adhesion locomotives
95 – 98	760-mm rack locomotives
99	600-mm adhesion locomotives

This brief history is sufficient for one to understand the reasons behind Yugoslavia's diversity of steam engines, but over the last decade a vast modernisation programme has been carried out including electrification of certain main lines, especially the one from Sežana to Belgrade, whilst a large number of American and other diesels have considerably reduced the country's steam inheritance. In view of this it is a great pity that much of the country is so hostile towards visiting enthusiasts – this especially applies in Serbia, Bosnia and Croatia, where the official attitude seems to be that steam is obsolescent, therefore best forgotten, and any foreigner delving into the history of such a subject is unwelcome. Another difficulty is that Yugoslavia's railways have military importance so that photography is forbidden altogether – a neurosis which is partly understandable when the country's position between eastern and western powers is considered, and the fact that it has seven different borders – including one with a

Chinese-orientated country! Another problem permanently bedevilling the nation is the extremist groups who still fight against the country's unity. I mention such points as a partial explanation of the country's hostility, but little can excuse Yugoslavia's uninterested and aggressive attitude towards those genuinely interested in its cultural and historical affairs. Despite months of fruitless negotiations little co-operation was forthcoming, and after a much maligned and persecuted stay in Serbia and Bosnia, during which I gleaned some hard-earned glimpses of the railway, I moved northwards to Slovenia where conditions were mercifully more tolerable. Luckily, this republic has much vintage steam, especially of the Austrian types, and I was fortunate to receive the help and companionship of Yugoslavia's

Yugoslavia

celebrated author Tadej Bratè. Our adventures together in filming Slovenian steam engines would fill many pages but suffice it to say that much of the Yugoslav nation's indifference towards documentation and preservation of this historical subject is greatly offset by Tadej Bratè's efforts.

Such impoverished thinking on behalf of this nation is not tempered by any traditions of railway enthusiasm in Yugoslavia for this is principally a phenomenon of the more sophisticated countries. Even today, Yugoslavia has a fascinating tapestry of steam types, some having long since become extinct in their native lands. Such a heritage puts responsibility on the country to preserve a representative selection and great credit must go to men like Tadej Bratè for their inspired awareness and achievements, amid so cool a climate of national indifference.

J.Z. standard 05/06 classes 4-6-2/2-8-2   Plate No. 59

These two classes are immensely important in Yugoslav railway history as being representative of the country's true standard locomotives. As previously mentioned, the greater proportion of Yugoslavia's motive power was inherited from other lands, as a result of both territorial changes and wartime reparations, and although certain basic types were absorbed into the J.Z. from the various constituent republics, especially those of Serbia with the famous 01 class 2-6-2 and 20 class 2-6-0, the overall power situation was made up of a motley collection of engines. Accordingly, Yugoslavia desperately needed some standard locomotives for working express passenger, express mixed traffic and heavy freight trains. This led to collaboration with Germany for the delivery in 1930 of three separate classes, each possessing identical boilers and tenders and many other standardised features. So came into being the 05 class Pacific for express passenger work, the 06 class 2-8-2 for mixed traffic duties and the 30 class 2-10-0 for heavy freight haulage. All were built with bar frames, superheaters and piston valves; the 05/06s having two cylinders whilst the 2-10-0 had three. These locomotives were considerably larger and more powerful than anything hitherto used upon Yugoslav territory, but their introduction came at a time when large sections of main line had been upgraded from the old 14/16-ton axle limits to over 19 tons, although certain sections had to be specially improved in order to accommodate the 2-10-0s.

The 05s, which came from Schwartzkopff's Works, became Yugoslavia's fastest steam engines, with a top speed of 62 m.p.h., and were put to work on the lightly-graded main lines, their principal duties being the 260-mile journey between Zagreb and Belgrade – the main line running through the heart of Yugoslavia – and the Belgrade–Niš–Skopje services. In comparison, the Borsig-built 06s worked the more difficult routes, like the Zagreb–Rijeka line, which runs through the Karst Mountains of Croatia, whilst they have also done much work on the steeply-graded lines around Ljubljana. The 30s worked in Serbia and Slovenia and on the Karst lines in Croatia and were the most powerful steam engines Yugoslavia ever had. Although immensely useful, they were very heavy on fuel and sometimes when they were working hard two firemen were required to maintain pressure. Altogether 110 locomotives of the three classes were delivered, the proportions being 30 06s, 40 05s and 40 30s.

Even in these classes we cannot discern anything which is typically Yugoslavian, for they are essentially German export locomotives, similar in overall appearance to others supplied to various Eastern European countries. However, they are typical products of the 1930s and possibly for this reason they seem to epitomise the latter-day travel agents' idea of a modern express steam locomotive, with their bold fronts dominated by immense smoke deflectors and tiny chimneys, making them just like many unrealistic drawings of ultra-modern steam locomotives. In point of fact the three types look remarkably similar, especially the 05/06s, which only differ visually in their wheel arrangement. The 30s do look considerably longer in the boiler – an illusion created by their five 4 ft $5\frac{1}{8}$-in.-diameter driving wheels – but the standard length for the three classes without their tenders is 44 ft. The plate clearly shows how high the boilers are pitched, and the firebox extends over the rear pair of coupled wheels rather than behind them.

Despite the satisfaction they gave, the standard classes were destined to have a shorter life than most J.Z. types, for during the 1960s an influx of American main line diesels severely depleted their ranks and ousted them from many top duties. Nowadays very few survive, the 05s being confined to certain turns around Niš in the south, whilst all remaining 06s are confined to Slovenia working from Maribor depot, from which their principal duty is mixed traffic work up the 12-mile line to the Austrian border at Spielfeld-Strass – part of the Belgrade–Vienna main line. Their operation on this line has provided many people with their first glimpse of Yugoslav steam as the 06s actually work over the border into Austria. This was my first experience of them in 1971 and what a contrast they made with the O.B.B.'s 52 class 2–10–0s (*Twilight of Steam,* plate 11) which stood alongside in Spielfeld station! Certainly the 06s heightened my desire to discover more of Yugoslavia's steam treasures, for their bold, stately appearance impressed me greatly as the engines rolled through the wooded countryside between Spielfeld and the border. One incongruity, however, is their strange high-pitched whistle which is at variance with the engines' aura of power. One would surely expect something more akin to the deep siren sound of Russian engines, though it might be said that such whistles do adequately distinguish the 06s from the deeper tones of ex-Austrian engines, amongst which they work on Slovenian soil. Whilst watching the class around Spielfeld I sensed what pre-grouping Britain must have been like when locomotives worked on to other companies' territories. Over the years we have read older enthusiasts' accounts of their thrill upon seeing these inter-company trespassers for the first time, bringing with them the magic and atmosphere of another school of thinking and practice, and I think with these 06s I sensed some of the excitement which true enthusiasts inevitably gain from such experiences. Handling international traffic over this section provided the 06s with some latter-day distinction, but during 1972 the accursed diesel began appearing upon intermittent trains, forcing more 06s either to withdrawal or onto the Maribor–Cakovec passenger trains, a duty which takes them over Maribor's river bridge which lies to the south (see plate 59). Also some 06s are ending their days on pick-up freight duties along the Bleiburg line – Maribor's other route into Austria.

It seems rather ironic that so few 06s were built when one considers that amongst the last steam locomotives constructed for the J.Z. were batches of Hungarian 4–8–0s (M.A.V. 424 class, J.Z. 11 class). Although similar engines in many respects, the M.A.V.s have an axle loading of only 14 tons, compared with the 06s' $17\frac{1}{2}$ tons. Nowadays, almost all Yugoslav steam is confined to secondary lines, rendering the heavy standards increasingly obsolescent, whilst the lighter Hungarian relations have flourished, the quantity owned by the J.Z. being greater than the 06 total.

Nevertheless, the 05/06/30s will go down in history as the only steam engines indigenous to the Yugoslav State Railways. Various differences occur within the 05/06 dimensions, the former having $22\frac{3}{4} \times 26$-in. cylinders, 6 ft $0\frac{3}{4}$-in. driving wheels and a $19\frac{1}{2}$-ton axle loading compared with the 06s' 2-in.-greater cylinder diameter, 5 ft 3-in. driving wheels and $17\frac{1}{2}$-ton axle loading. Their common boilers give them a pressure of 227 lbs per sq. in. and a 54.2 sq. ft grate area, whilst their total engine weights in full working order are 98 and 100 tons respectively. One trusts that the Yugoslav nation will have the presence of mind to preserve one standard engine, if only in deference to some stability amongst the turmoil of the past.

J.Z. 17 class 2–6–2T
Plate Nos. 6, 7, 10

It was a scorching hot afternoon as I sat in the Slovenian country-side with Tadej Bratè, an afternoon which seemed to bear out Yugo-slavia's oft-repeated designation of 'sunny'. Our cameras were at the ready as we waited beside the railway near Most na Soči on a line which carried locomotives descended from various European families. It was a wonderful experience to converse and film with this almost solitary Yugoslavian enthusiast for, quite apart from his knowledge of Yugoslav engines, his uninhibited enthusiasm was a constant inspira-tion. We had calculated that the next train along this exciting line would be a passenger, hauled by an ex-Hungarian 2–6–2T belonging to the J.Z. 17 class. There was time to wait and Tadej began to discuss the 17s, explaining how they were originally built to supersede the smaller Hungarian 375 class (see plate 14) on suburban duties around Budapest. The first two were introduced in 1915 as the 342 class, being considerably larger than the 375s with 5 ft $3\frac{1}{4}$-in.-diameter driving wheels for greater speed. These two engines created a precedent for a further 295 examples, 145 from Henschel and 150 from Budapest over the years 1916–18. Typically Hungarian in appearance, the 342s became a standard in that country and formed a basis for the M.A.V.'s later 442 class 2–8–2Ts, which also worked around Budapest for many years.

So often during our conversations on European engines I would ask Tadej how the first ones of a class came to Yugoslavia. Of course, he lost no time in telling me how Yugoslavia took Croatia from the Austrian Empire in 1918 and how with it came eighty-six 342 class tank engines. At the same time Roumania took a large part of Hungary, so receiving 109 engines, whilst another five went to Czecho-slovakia, leaving rather less than 100 in the much-diminished Hungary. Upon absorbing them, the S.H.S. retained the M.A.V.'s classification of 342 until, under the later J.D.Z. scheme, they became the 17 class. Tadej continued by telling how they had largely been used over the flatter areas in Croatia on secondary mixed traffic work. The further three which came to Yugoslavia after World War II brought the J.D.Z. numbers up to eighty-nine.

No sooner had we set this into perspective than the throb of a distant train was heard and a dusky smoke trail could be seen rising up over the distant fields. Sure enough it was the 17 and thus it was with enlightened vision that I viewed this Hungarian locomotive and I hope that plate No. 10 conveys the atmosphere of that moment. One of the most interesting things I learned about this class was that they had Brotan boilers, for when the 17 had gone I received an animated lecture from Tadej as he drew out the technicalities of this innovation in the lineside dust with the aid of a stick. Apparently when built most 342s possessed Brotan boilers. He explained that Hungary's available coal had a high sulphur content and this created a bad effect on copper firebox plates, so the Brotan boiler was developed whereby the firebox sides were formed of vertical steel water tubes leading to a steam drum at the top, the tubes being encased outside by a lagged firebrick layer. The innovation was not as strong as a traditional firebox whilst furthermore the firebrick casing often became out of condition and caused air leaks which affected combustion. It is believed that around 1,000 engines received Brotan boilers, many of them Hungarian. As Tadej pointed out, the Brotan 17s have their steam collection dome above the firebox steam drum, whereas the non-Brotan engines have their steam domes in a central position with their feed water cleaner drums fitted above the firebox (note the silhouette on plates 6 and 7). This device is typical of Hungarian locomotives as they invariably sport huge cylindrical water cleaners and these, along with separate sand and steam collection domes, combined with a flared backing plate behind the chimney, result in a very rugged boiler appearance.

We were still discussing the 17s when the next train came along headed by an ex-Austrian 0–10–0, J.Z. 28 class, an engine type which shares the odd passenger train workings with the 17s between Jesenice and Sežana. Tadej went on to say that only about thirty 17 class engines remained and although they only came to Slovenia during the late 1930s all survivors are now concentrated there. Some may still be found in Roumania and also in their land of origin where certain engines have received adjusted weight distribution for increased adhesion and been reclassified 315 by the M.A.V.

An intrinsic care for both the aesthetic and technical aspects of steam must invariably render its study more worthwhile and it was no small experience to be amid such fine locomotives while intimately studying their histories in the company of so celebrated an expert. By the end of the day we had bagged a fine selection of pictures and I found it hard to believe that European steam was near to extinction.

The 17s' leading dimensions are: cylinders $19\frac{1}{2}$ in × $25\frac{1}{2}$ in, driving wheel diameter 5 ft $3\frac{1}{4}$ in., boiler pressure 185 lbs per sq. in. and grate area $25\frac{1}{4}$ sq. ft. Their axle loading is 14 tons and total weight in full working order 71 tons.

J.Z. 18 class 4–6–2T   Plate Nos. 24, 58

One of the most interesting classes I found in Yugoslavia was these splendid ex-Austrian 4–6–2Ts. Only five of them went to the Yugoslav Railways, being part of a larger consignment of reparation engines, including various classes, received by the J.Z. after World War II. The Yugoslavs classified them 18 with the numbers 001–005. At present, all five are still extant at Maribor and employed on passenger duties along the 58-mile Bleiburg line – a duty which actually takes them back into their former territory, as Bleiburg lies just inside the Austrian border. This scenic branch line provides one with 18s on passenger and 25s/06s on freight, and during my week's stay in the area I became increasingly fond of these typically Austrian tanks. Their gaunt angular outline signifies an applaudable vintage which is accentuated by the tall stovepipe chimney, Austrian-style smokebox door, low side tanks and large driving wheels – a combination of elements which, for me, puts this class amongst the most exciting of European steam engines. A handful still survive in their native land working suburban trains around Vienna (Nord), but the appearance of these engines has been totally ruined by the incorporation of Giesl Ejectors.

My filming of the 18s at Maribor was memorable and one afternoon I was sitting by the river when two of them backed over the bridge coupled together, one running in after extensive repairs. I knew that one was scheduled to work the afternoon passenger to Bleiburg, but it occurred to me that the two engines might double-head the train. Eagerly I raced down to the station and there, sure enough, were the two 18s on the head of a four-coach train, the two antiques smokily simmering in readiness whilst their crews completed oiling up. I had just enough time to get into position near the viaduct to film their departure. With both engines emitting dense clouds of exhaust they crossed the water and headed away westwards. It is capturing such rare

179

sights as this that counterbalances the innumerable problems involved in successful railway photography – especially in communist countries!

During that week I had further adventures with the 18s, for one was timed to leave Maribor at dusk and it became my custom to film the train leaving and then, after a hectic drive, see it again at Rûse, ten miles up the line. The train was allowed twenty-four minutes for this distance, which of course included a number of stops, but I had to drive ten miles, including a lengthy exit through Maribor's suburbs. It was always a tense chase and upon approaching Rûse the 18's exhaust trail could invariably be seen approaching as the train traversed Slovenia's rolling countryside. That I sometimes succeeded in catching the train is testified by plate 24 and in this study I feel that something of the 18s' magnificence has been captured. Also at Rûse I saw an ex-Austrian State Railway 2-6-0 compound tank with double-dome-handle boiler (OBB 91 class – see *Twilight of Steam*). This gem was working from a factory adjacent to the station.

The 18s first appeared in 1913 on Austria's Sudbahn Railway as the 629 class, with fifteen engines being built between 1913 and 1915, and the design was perpetuated by the Austrian State Railway, K.K.St.B., from 1917 onwards. Unlike many Austrian engines of that period, the class was a two-cylinder superheated simple and proved ideal for both cross-country and suburban work. Their 13-ton axle loading gave these powerful and speedy engines a wide route availability and after Austria's railways were united, construction continued under the Austrian Federal Railways, B.B.O., until 1927, by which time 100 629s had been built, some with larger side tanks. Five engines received Caprotti Valve Gear, whilst twenty-five had Lentz Valves, and in more recent years some engines were fitted with water-softening apparatus. During the Nazi occupation of Austria the 629s became absorbed into D.R.B. stock, being reclassified 77^2, and upon Austria's regaining its former identity they became known as the 77 class. In Austrian traditions the 629s might be regarded as forerunners of the O.B.B. 78 4-6-4Ts (see *Twilight of Steam,* page 174).

After the Austrian Empire was split up in 1918, some fifteen 629s found their way onto Czechoslovakian territory, and the class's satisfactory operation determined the Czechs to continue building. Accordingly, 1922 saw Skoda producing almost identical engines and they became standards on the Czechoslovakian State Railway (C.S.D.), and building continued until 1941. Czechoslovakia now possesses the majority, which run as the C.S.D. 354.1 class. Some C.S.D. engines were built with double-dome-handle boilers – a feature which the Austrian engines never had, and one received Lentz Valves during Czechoslovakia's experimentation with this system. Others worked on both Hungarian and Polish territory but none survives there today.

The 18s' principal dimensions are: cylinders $18\frac{3}{4}$ in. × $28\frac{3}{8}$ in., driving wheel diameter 5 ft 2 in., boiler pressure 185 lbs per sq. in., grate area 29 sq. ft and total weight in full working order, 79 tons.

Whilst seeing 18s at work in Yugoslavia I inevitably drew comparisons both historically and aesthetically with the J.Z. 17 class 2–6–2Ts (ex-Hungarian 342 class) which also operate cross-country passenger trains in Slovenia. This class is discussed on page 177. One of the original Sudbahn engines is scheduled to be preserved in Austria's Railway Museum.

J.Z. 25 class 2–8–0   Plate Nos. 38, 39, 57

Shortly before 5.00 a.m. we drove out of Ljubljana just as the first workers of this modern town were stirring. I was accompanied by Tadej Bratė and with food and equipment stowed away we headed for a two day visit to the remote and little-known Kočevje line. As we left Ljubljana the glorious Slovenian countryside welled up around us with Tadej incessantly pointing out interesting features – although needless to say, our conversation never veered far from steam locomotives. Our mission was to film the J.Z. 25 class, relics from a 75-year-old line of Austrian Empire 2–8–0s. All Yugoslav survivors were centered upon Slovenia, many around Ljubljana, and very early each morning no less than three took freights down the rickety single line to Kočevje, and it was with the intention of catching one that we had started so early. As the journey progressed, the countryside became increasingly wild and the tiny wayside villages, in which time seemed to stand still, became fewer and fewer. Eventually we turned off the main road and headed over rough country tracks to reach this lonely branch line until, amid a cloud of dust and scattering chickens, we drew up outside an old station. Tadej leapt out to confer about the trains and returning almost immediately said with a beaming smile 'Two gone, one to come – and she's got a big train!'

With cameras over our shoulders, we set off down the rusty, weed-grown metals to photograph the locomotive as it approached. For Tadej it was just another 25, and he knew them well, if he did not actually take them for granted; after all they have worked in Slovenia for almost fifty years. But for me it was to be a first glimpse of a living link with the pages of locomotive history and as we walked that lonely branch line my mind was on the 25s' creator, the famous Dr. Golsdorf, Chief Mechanical Engineer of the Austrian State Railways from 1891 to 1916, a man credited with some sixty steam locomotive designs and the creator of a vast family of locomotives, the very last remnants of which may still be found in various parts of Europe. Today such distinctive families of engines become increasingly valuable as more standardised and universal types become prominent amongst steam's ever-diminishing ranks.

Although they were not built until just after Golsdorf's death, it is to him that the 25s are credited, owing to their being direct descendants of his 170 class two-cylinder compound 2–8–0s, introduced in 1897. Almost 900 of these compounds were built, including some for the Austrian Sudbahn Railway and for Czechoslovakia, with building continuing until 1919. Golsdorf was a great believer in both big engines and compounding, for during his tenure of office he graduated in a 20-year period from two-cylinder compound 0–6–0s to four-cylinder compound 2–12–0s, his 170 class being part of this progression. However, the advent of superheating caused a change of policy and in 1917, the year after Golsdorf's death, a superheated simple version of the 170 came out. Classified 270, these were the engines which now make up the J.Z. 25 class. Perhaps Tadej interpreted my thoughts, for he suddenly mentioned how widespread the 270s became, since of the 500 or so built many were delivered new to Poland, Hungary, Czechoslovakia and Yugoslavia, whilst the breaking up of the Austrian Empire saw others pass to Italy and Roumania. Building continued up to 1930.

The type first came to Yugoslavia when the S.H.S. ordered nine ostensibly new engines from Weiner Neustadt, Vienna. These were Austrian Military Railway reserve stocks, having previously been built between 1919 and 1923 but never used. The S.H.S. also classified them 270 and employed them in Slovenia on various duties, including the operation of fast trains. About twenty-five more came to Slovenia after World War II, so bringing the Yugoslav total to around thirty-five engines. Tadej informed me that only five of these have been cut up, the others still working secondary lines throughout the Slovenian Republic.

A mournful wail resounded through the woods and Tadej, in typical broken English, cried 'She comes – and she's making plenty smoke!'

Sure enough, the 25 came into view, with the morning sunshine gleaming on her ornate Austrian-style smokebox doors. (Sadly many of these have now been removed in favour of the more modern kind.) Never had I experienced such an engine, the tiny chimney and huge cylinders looking almost comical, although it must be added that this was not the orignal chimney, as the Yugoslavs have reduced them by some 6-in. for working under electrification wires. Nevertheless her appearance was typically Austrian, the dome shape being gloriously moulded. I found it difficult to appreciate immediately a design so alien to the British traditions I had always been accustomed to. It takes some time for one to become at home with locomotives of new outlines – rather like the face of a new acquaintance, strange at first, but after a while blossoming out into complete familiarity. The 25 stopped in the yard for a time, so enabling me to inspect the wheezy creature a little further as it shunted the small siding, until after collecting its train together it headed away again through the woods.

We took up chase, and some high speed driving along rough, dusty roads enabled us to overtake the 25 momentarily, but when it whirled its train onto a long downgrade section it drew into the lead again and finally disappeared out of sight further ahead. To Tadej's persistent 'Keep on driving', we bounced along, seemingly on two wheels, and after the vibrations and swirling dust had put me into a stupor, we managed to catch the 25 further on, just as she was preparing to leave another station yard. Frantically we leapt from the vehicle and like men possessed tore down the track ahead of the train, to the incredulous gazes of the station staff. With the 25 hard on our heels, and flinging up a fantastically rich brown exhaust, we ran on. 'To the signal', I yelled at Tadej. The sound of the approaching engine drew closer until we stumbled past the signal and turned to face the oncoming train. I was almost too exhausted and excited to work my camera but limply aiming it at the engine bearing down upon us, I obtained plate 39. Satisfied by this rare study, we voted ourselves 'out for the count' and decided to proceed at a more leisurely pace on to Kočevje.

'What an engine!' was all I could say to Tadej, and his agreement led him on to say how he knew every surviving 25 individually, by adornments such as the varying kinds of brass rings around their chimneys, the various kinds and sizes of chimney, with or without backing plates, and many other slight details, such as tender-cabs. The class's chimneys were of rather hybrid form, for apart from their being cut down in size, various kinds of new ones have been added, as the original Austrian ones burned through.

Upon reaching Kočevje we found the three 25s all in the goods yard and Tadej pointed out one engine which had a chimney backing plate. This device, which rather alters the locomotive's appearance, allegedly lifts smoke and sparks clear from the driver's view, but only a few engines are fitted at random and it was Tadej's considered opinion that neither the J.Z. authorities nor the enginemen knew whether it was effective or not. Only two trains were scheduled back to Ljubljana, which meant that one train would have a 25 on either end, and after a wait of several hours we were rewarded by the sight of the first train leaving with two 25s. Plate 38 was made as the train headed away from the town.

My two days with these engines were full of poignant memories: sunshine, deep blue skies, swirling motion, rattling brown wagons, wooded hills and decrepit wayside stations with rusty, weed-strewn sidings, all combined with the haunting whistles of this lovely breed as they acted out their final drama. Tadej does much liaison work with Slovenia's Technical Museum and several times he said 'You know, we must preserve one somehow. I must see what I can do.' Of course, I became a verbal accomplice to such sentiment, despite the fact that several are already preserved! One of the original 170 compounds is restored in Czechoslovakia, whilst a few still work in Austria on the G.K.B. colliery system at Graz, and it is also intended to preserve one of these. In common with all Golsdorf products, the 270s are now extinct on the Austrian Federal Railways, although one has been set by for preservation. Later on my tour I was to encounter the 25s again at Maribor and plate 57 depicts one smokily ambling its way over the viaduct en route to the sheds.

Dimensions are as follows:

	Original 170 compounds, 1897	Developed 270 simples, 1917
Cylinders: H.P.	$21\frac{1}{4}$ in. × $24\frac{3}{4}$ in.	$22\frac{1}{2}$ in. × $24\frac{3}{4}$ in.
Cylinders: L.P.	$31\frac{1}{2}$ in. × $24\frac{3}{4}$ in.	
Driving wheel diameter	4 ft $1\frac{1}{2}$ in.	4 ft $1\frac{1}{2}$ in.
Boiler pressure	171 lbs per sq. in.	185 lbs per sq. in.
Grate area	42 sq. ft	42 sq. ft
Axle loading	14 tons	14 tons
Total weight of engine (without tender)	68 tons	68 tons

The origin of these engines may be traced to the turn of the century on the Austrian State Railways when, in his quest for a more powerful freight engine, their engineer Karl Golsdorf produced a kind of *magnum opus* with his magnificent 180 class two-cylinder compound 0–10–0s of 1900, forerunners of the locomotives illustrated. Originally built for the Klostergrab–Moldan line in Bohemia, and for other sinuous lines throughout Austria, the 180s' 13.1-ton axle loading was light for so powerful an engine, notwithstanding all their 66 ton weight being available for adhesion. The sinuosity of Austria's railways made production of an 0–10–0 difficult, but Golsdorf overcame this problem by allowing considerable side play in the axles. However, since side play was difficult to achieve on the driving axle, Golsdorf incorporated fourth-axle drive, so giving the centrally-placed third axle lateral action. All 180s used saturated steam and many possessed double-dome-handle boilers, although some later engines were fitted with steam driers and accordingly had only one dome. But the class's most interesting characteristic was their immense $33\frac{1}{2}$-in.-diameter low-pressure cylinder for, as can be imagined, these gave a remarkably weird shape to the front end. Over 200 180s were built, including twenty-seven for the Austrian Sudbahn Railway, and they were destined to operate in Czechoslovakia, Poland and Yugoslavia.

After about a decade Golsdorf introduced an improved 180 with his 80 class superheated compounds. These had piston valves on their high pressure cylinders although some later ones possessed piston valves for both cylinders. Building continued in this form up to about 150 engines until in 1916 the final graduation to superheated simples with piston valves was reached, being classified 80.9. The three variants mentioned were similar in appearance and typical of transitions from saturated compound to superheated simples undertaken by many railways upon the advent of superheating. Over 400 80.9s were built, many going new to Poland, Roumania, Hungary and Greece, whilst some also went to the Sudbahn Railway.

Having looked briefly at the origins of this prolific Austrian class, let us see how they came to Yugoslavia. The story began in 1907 when six 180 class engines were ordered by the Serbian State Railways for their mountainous line between Belgrade and Velika Plana. But it is in Slovenia that the type really belongs, for when this area was taken from Austria after 1918, the S.H.S. inherited about three dozen 180s, 80s and 80.9s. Then in 1927 the S.H.S. supplemented these by ordering ten new 80.9s from Weiner Neustadt, Vienna. These engines had been built in 1923 as Austrian Military Reserve stock, and accordingly they were sold at a competitive price. A further four engines were similarly commissioned from Austria in 1929. Thus these 0–10–0s worked on Yugoslav soil until after World War II, when they were augmented by a further thirty engines, of both 80 and 80.9 varieties, which were left in Slovenia after the occupation. These came from Austria and Poland whilst others, taken from the Italians, were engines received by Italy after World War I. This gave the J.D.Z. around sixty-seven examples. A policy of converting the compounds into 80.9 simples was undertaken, and the few compounds which survived this rebuilding have since been broken up. Under the Yugoslav classification scheme all engines became the 28 class. This rebuilding was undertaken partly because the excessive size of the low-pressure cylinder put greater weight on one side, so rendering the engines rather unstable. On the subject of stability, the Yugoslavs have frequently used two 28s double-headed on express passenger trains in Istria, with speeds frequently exceeding 50 m.p.h., although of course their duties were principally hauling heavy freights. They have remained true to their origins in Slovenia and even today around fifteen of these trojans can be seen slogging their way across the Slovenian landscape with such an aura of pugnacity that one can never imagine them stalling. For a short time one engine was experimentally fitted with a Giesl ejector.

I always associate these Austrian 0–10–0s with Štanjel, for I loved the way they smokily fought their way up to the summit (see plate 12). I stayed at Štanjel over several wonderfully happy days enjoying the unique atmosphere of an all-steam railway. Štanjel is something of a magical place for, quite apart from the railway itself, the village, which is of Roman origin, stands on a hill at the head of a valley. Trains from Nova Gorica climb through this valley before entering a tunnel under the hill to come into Štanjel station. The hill, village, and distant tunnel may be seen on plate 60. I have called this picture 'Living History' as it combines a Roman village with an Austrian Empire locomotive on German-built Krupp rails of 1887 vintage.

During filming I received much hospitality from the inhabitants of this village and they told me that during the Middle Ages Štanjel had been a very important trading town between Italy and Austria. During

World War II the village was badly damaged through battles between the Partisans and Germans in 1944, when the Partisans were scattered and many of Štanjel's inhabitants were sent away to concentration camps. Nowadays artists come here to paint. The Slovenian authorities intend to develop Štanjel as a tourist attraction by restoring its castle and 400-year-old church, but when this comes about one can be sure that these wonderful 0–10–0s will no longer be present. So as some of Štanjel's history returns to prevalence another aspect will irretrievably pass into obscurity.

Over part of my stay there I was with Tadej Bratè and never will I forget the long chases we made with these 28s as they climbed through the valley. In the sweltering heat we pursued them for mile after mile and arrived at Štanjel soaked with sweat to assuage ourselves with the cool joys of the station water pump. Through Tadej's efforts, a 28 is to be preserved in Slovenia. She is to be restored to original Austrian condition with taller chimney and spark arrester, along with other detail changes, such as reduced tender coal space. A truly handsome exhibit will result. Tadej managed to achieve this preservation agreement after much battling and his success constitutes a real triumph against the blithe indifference of many Yugoslav railway officials towards steam's history. A 180 class compound with original two-dome boiler graces the Technical Museum in Vienna, whilst the Austrians have also set by an 80.9 simple for preservation. Another 180 is to be preserved in Italy, being one of the class which worked there after World War II.

The comparative dimensions of this enthralling succession of 0–10–0s is set out below.

	Original 180 saturated compound	Intermediate 80 superheated compound	Final 80.9 superheated simple
Cylinders: H.P.	22 in. × 24¾ in.	23¼ in. × 24¾ in.	23¼ in. × 24¾ in.
Cylinders: L.P.	33½ in. × 24¾ in.	33½ in. × 24¾ in. 3	
Driving wheel diameter	4 ft 1½ in.	4 ft 1½ in.	4 ft 1½ in.
Boiler pressure	185 lbs per sq. in.	199 lbs per sq. in.	199 lbs per sq. in.
Grate area	36½ sq. ft	36½ sq. ft	36½ sq. ft
Total weight in working order (Engine only)	66 tons	70 tons	70 tons

As stated earlier, the royalist government of Yugoslavia declared allegiance to Germany in 1941, much against the national will; this led to an uprising and the government was overthrown. Following this, Germany attacked Belgrade by air on 6 April 1941 with the result that Yugoslavia was forced to capitulate and the country was divided. Much of northern Yugoslavia was taken by Italy, Germany and Hungary, whilst a new Croatian state was formed and Serbia passed to German rule. This created the Croatian State Railways (H.D.Z.) and the Serbian State Railways (C.D.Z.). It was to these two administrations that the first German 52 class Kriegslok War Engines were delivered on Yugoslav soil, when in 1943-4 the H.D.Z. received twenty-five new engines, followed by the C.D.Z. with fifteen in 1944. The C.D.Z. classified them 33, whilst those in Croatia became the 30 class, so bringing them into line with Yugoslavia's standard 30 class 2-10-0 (see page 174). After the war the reconstituted J.Z. adopted Serbia's classification of 33 and the 40 locomotives were absorbed as numbers 001-40.

The end of the war brought a considerable surplus of Kriegsloks and, owing to their power and light 15-ton axle loading, the type was thought ideal for Yugoslavia as a cheaply-obtained new standard type. Accordingly, the J.Z. purchased some 220 from Germany and the class quickly spread into most republics. Over more recent years, Yugoslavia bought a further seventy-five examples from Russia, so bringing the J.Z. total of 33s to little short of 350 engines. The Germans had used their Kriegsloks during the attempted conquest of Russia, with a result that about 1,500 were taken by Russia, reclassified T3 and converted to their 5 ft 0 in. gauge by adjustment of the cylinders and frames and provision of longer axles. Although quite a number still remain in Russia today, many have since been reconverted to standard gauge and sold to various East European countries. Yugoslavia decided to purchase this later batch of Kriegsloks in order to replace the less powerful American S160 2-8-0s (J.Z. 37 class). Today the 33s are Yugoslavia's most numerous steam type and may still be found in most areas. Thus they have become far more important than the J.Z. standard 30 class 2-10-0 of 1930.

Considering Yugoslavia's role in the upheavals of recent European history, it was inevitable that the country should acquire a liberal smattering of Kriegsloks, for these engines have almost become Europe's standard freight engine. An incredible total of almost 6,500 was built and if we consider the basic D.R.B. 50 class 2–10–0 of 1938, from which the Kriegslok was developed in 1942, a grand total of some 10,000 examples existed. The 50 class 2–10–0 (see *Twilight of Steam,* page 122) graduated into the Kriegslok via a series of modifications designed to save man hours and using non-ferrous metals; this created the class 50 U.K., which means 'Übergangs-Kriegslokomotiven' or 'transitional war engine'.

The Kriegslok proper was, of course, the true Austerity and in order to facilitate rapid production, both in Germany and in the works of occupied countries, emphasis was placed upon ease of construction combined with a reduction in the use of short supply materials – many parts being made by various outside factories. The resultant engines had such characteristics as a lack of deflector plates, a fabricated motion, welded steel firebox, and no top feed dome or feed water heater, whilst many had plate frames. Their welded tenders were specially designed without an underframe, the main structure simply resting upon two bogies. In order to achieve this, a semi-circular design had to be prepared and this, which is one of the class's most interesting features, carried 7,000 gallons of water and 10 tons of coal. In September 1942 the first was steamed and construction proceeded at a rate of about 2,600 per annum over the ensuing two-and-a-half years, with building being undertaken in Germany, Austria, Poland, France and Belgium. The essential dimensions of the 50/52s were virtually identical. In the summer of 1943, the Germans produced a more powerful Austerity in their 42 class 2–10–0, which had an axle load of $17\frac{1}{4}$ tons and was designed for operating the heavier lines throughout Germany's occupied territories.

As mentioned earlier, the immense number of Kriegsloks, combined with the distribution, both during wartime and as post-war reparations, rendered them a standard European type, for they appeared in almost every European country. Even Russia's 5 ft 0 in. gauge was not to deter them. Today, thirty years after their inception, these German warriors march on throughout half of Europe, especially amongst the Eastern European countries, and the many variations which now occur within their ranks make them a fascinating study. The greatest variation appears in East Germany where many have been rebuilt with new standard boilers interchangeable with the D.R. 23[10] class 2–6–2, 50 class 2–10–0 and ex-Prussian G12. Yugoslavia has contributed some embellishments, if only the addition of German-style smoke deflectors smartly adorned with painted flags. These, combined with a high standard of cleanliness amongst the 33s, make them a highly impressive looking locomotive, especially when one takes into consideration their attractive semi-circular tenders.

Although widely distributed throughout much of Yugoslavia, the 33s are a recent addition in Slovenia, which has traditionally used older ex-Austrian classes. But a few years ago the Slovenian authorities decided to purchase a batch of 33s which had become redundant in order to replace some of their older ex-Prussian G12 2–10–0s. The 33s were assigned to Nova Gorica depot for operation on the Jesenice–Sežana line, but unfortunately they proved to be too long for the turntables and have to be operated tender-first when running northwards – this can be seen in plate 55. In this respect it seems a shame that Slovenia could not have purchased some Vulcan *Liberations*, many of which also lay redundant, as these are sufficiently short to allow turning. Whether the Slovenians were ignorant of the *Liberations*' existence, or whether their axle loads were too high is in question, but I do understand that when the 33s were purchased no-one realised that they could not be turned. Had the *Liberations* come to Slovenia, it would have atoned my long fruitless wait for them on the Banja Luka–Doboj line – a route which I erroneously calculated to be *Liberation* worked. Despite this it was good to see the Kriegsloks in Slovenia, even if only to provide a reminder that in the mid-1970s Europe still possesses a standard steam freight engine.

In setting out the 33s' dimensions it will be interesting to compare them with their British counterparts, the lesser-known Riddles Ministry of Supply Austerity 2–10–0s, which Britain built from 1943 for service on the Western Front.

	D.R.B. '52' Kriegslok 2–10–0	M.O.S. Riddles 2–10–0
Cylinders	$23\frac{5}{8}$ in. × 26 in.	19 in. × 28 in.
Boiler pressure	227 lbs per sq. in.	225 lbs per sq. in.
Driving wheel diameter	4 ft 7 in.	4 ft $8\frac{1}{2}$ in.
Grate area	42 sq. ft	40 sq. ft
Axle loading	15 tons	$13\frac{1}{2}$ tons
Tractive effort 85% b.p.	50,930 lbs	34,215 lbs
Total weight of engine without tender	$83\frac{1}{4}$ tons	$78\frac{1}{2}$ tons

See also *Twilight of Steam,* page 128.

190

Immediately prior to the unification of Germany's railways the Prussians made an impressive variety of freight classes – primarily 0–8–0s, 0–10–0s and 2–10–0s. Amongst the most important were the G8' 0–8–0s introduced in 1913 from Hanomag, with superheaters, piston valves and Walschaerts valve gear, over 5,000 being built up to 1921. Almost simultaneously the G10 0–10–0s appeared having boilers identical with those of the P8 standard 4–6–0s, (see *Twilight of Steam,* page 124) and like the P8s, these 0–10–0s were destined to reach a total of around 3,500 engines.

Shortly before World War I broke out, Henschels were assigned to the task of producing a 2–10–0 of greater power than the G10s, and this led to the appearance of the G12' 2–10–0, a splendid three-cylinder affair with an axle load of $16\frac{1}{2}$ tons. Meantime, however, current wartime needs demanded the same power, but with a lighter axle loading, and so was born the G12 2–10–0 proper, the *pièce de rèsistance* among Prussian freight engines which, through careful manipulation of design, was given an axle load of only 15.7 tons for an even greater power output. In contrast with most other German locomotives, the G12s had Belpair fireboxes in accordance with current Prussian practice, whilst other interesting features were the use of bar-frames and conjugated valve gear to operate the middle cylinder. Over the following seven years 1,200 G12s were built, not only for Prussia, but also for the state railways of Baden, Saxony, and Wurttemburg. Unlike their relations the G8'/G10s, the G12s appeared rather late for a widespread European distribution after World War I, although Poland, which took much of Prussia's territory, received some and designated them Ty-1.

Upon absorption into the D.R.B. the G12s became reclassified 58[10] and continued to do excellent work throughout Germany although further construction work was thwarted by the advent of the three-cylinder 44 class 2–10–0 which appeared in 1927. As a result of the second war G12s became widely distributed throughout Europe whilst of course they were further split between East and West Germany, and it was during Germany's reparations to Yugoslavia that forty-nine examples were handed over. These the J.Z. reclassified 36 and num-bered 001–49. Excepting the J.Z. 30 class 2–10–0s, these 36s proved to be Yugoslavia's most powerful freight class, and they were a welcome supplement to the many older and less powerful two-cylinder Austrian types which handled much of the Yugoslav freight traffic. In 1961 a 36 class engine was chosen for tests with Giesl ejectors and although this proved to be extremely beneficial, it was by this time decided not to spend money on improvement to steam, but rather to conserve all available funds for modernisation. Thus a 36 became one of the very few Yugoslav engines to incorporate a Giesl fitting. By 1972, the original forty-nine engines had dwindled to about ten working survivors, all based at Nova Gorica depot in Slovenia for operating freight over the steeply-graded route between Jesenice and Sežana.

It was in Yugoslavia that I first became acquainted with a G12. It was night-time and upon driving past a freight yard near Nova Gorica, I observed a tell-tale plume of steam rising up above the wagons. Immediate investigation proved what I had hoped – that it was a 36 – and I became temporarily overawed by this majestic giant of Prussian history. I was beckoned into the warm, copious cabin to be greeted by an incommunicable flurry of the Yugoslav tongue and although I could do little but smile, no language was necessary when the driver opened the firebox door and showed the tremendous interior. I was astounded by the size, for although the actual grate area is only 42 sq. ft the box's long narrow design makes it appear immense. This memorable introduction to the G12s proved to be the first of many successive days spent with them on the Nova Gorica–Sežana line, a section which includes the 8-mile climb from Prvačina up to Štanjel summit.

In addition I was fortunate to have Tadej Bratè with me for part of the time, and upon reaching the bank later the same evening this inveterate enthusiast, with the skill of a native guide, directed me to a superb camp base just north of Štanjel summit. Through the darkness the trains rumbled by, including one hauled by the G12 we had seen earlier, and quite apart from calling out each type as soon as it became audible, Tadej almost knew which individual engine it was, and throughout our subsequent travels together he accurately identified individual engines from considerable distances. When morning finally came the procession of veterans steamed by like the fulfilment of an ephemeral and treasured dream and although there are many places where steam can be enjoyed, few lines offer such diverse vintage as Austrian 0–10–0s, Hungarian 2–6–2Ts, Prussian 2–10–0s and German War Engine 2–10–0s. Of course the G12s' three-cylinder rhythms differed considerably from the two-cylinder engines and vividly reminded me of the days when three-cylinder engines roamed many parts of Britain.

It became our practice to follow the trains as they smokily laboured their way up the bank from Prvačina, the line poignantly recalling the halcyon days of steam whilst additionally providing a treasured glance into the bowels of locomotive history. Plate 11 was made close to our base and it is interesting to note that the bridge under which the G12 is passing is heavily inscribed 'Erected under the Allied Military Government — 13 Corps during the British/American Occupation 1946'!

Some years have passed since the G12s disappeared from their West German haunts, but a number still survive in East Germany under their old D.R.B. classification 58. These have been rebuilt with new standard boilers and tenders, whilst their conjugated valve gear has been removed in favour of an extra set of Walschaerts. The class's principal dimensions are: three cylinders $22\frac{1}{2}$ in. × 26 in., driving wheels 4 ft $7\frac{1}{8}$-in. diameter, boiler pressure 199 lbs per sq. in., grate area 42 sq. ft. The engines' total weight in full working order is 91 tons.

Vulcan Liberations, J.Z. 38 class 2-8-0   Plate No. 13

In order to help supplement losses incurred during wartime and get countries back on their feet again after World War II, large numbers of locomotives were supplied by both Britain and America to various European countries under the U.N.R.R.A. scheme – United Nations Relief and Rehabilitation Administration. Many different types were included in the scheme, perhaps the best known being Major Marsh's classic American S160 2-8-0s of 1942, but Britain's principal contribution was the 110 Vulcan Liberations. These historic engines were built after collaboration with engineers from seven different countries and came from the Vulcan Foundry's Works at Newton le Willows, Lancs. Officially known as the Liberations, these 2-8-0s were expressly designed to play a role in the great liberation of Europe, as it was then known, although of course today the word liberation has somewhat more delicate connotations than it did in those traumatic times of twenty-five years ago! Yugoslavia was the biggest recipient, with sixty-five engines, whilst thirty went to Poland, becoming the Tr 202 class. The remaining fifteen were delivered to Czechoslovakia. Although only 2-8-0s, the Liberations were immensely powerful and their axle loading of $18\frac{1}{2}$ tons suited them to post-war European conditions. They were considerably more powerful than the S160s, which had originally been designed to suit the British loading gauge, but owing to their vast superiority in numbers, the S160s are still prevalent in many countries today. The Liberations were superheated engines with plate frames and copper fireboxes and were remarkably American looking, being not dissimilar to the S160s, yet despite their un-British appearance these squat, chunky engines possessed considerable character. Concurrent with the productions for U.N.R.R.A., Vulcan received an order for ten of the type from Luxembourg's National Railway and these additional engines were sold privately outside the U.N.R.R.A. contract, so bringing the actual total constructed to 120.

When built, the Liberations had an attractive plate symbolising the world set into their cab sides, with U.N.R.R.A.'s initials placed through the centre. Classified by U.N.R.R.A. 1D on the continental axle system, the Liberations were numbered 1D 1–110. Yugoslavia's

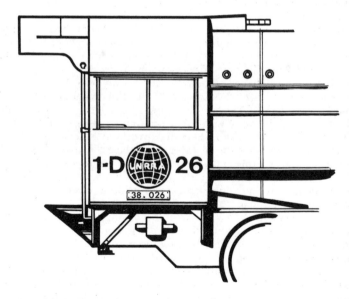

JZ 38 class 2–8–0 cab

consignment have retained both their 'worlds' and U.N.R.R.A. numbers, the J.Z. number simply being placed beneath as in the adjacent sketch. Also U.N.R.R.A.'s initials have been retained on the tenders and it is truly remarkable that such embellishments should have survived, as they can have little functional significance today, the class's J.Z. designation being 38.001–065. Delightful as these characteristics might be, one thing that has marred the class's appearance has been the extensions applied to the tender coal area, which give the originally handsome eight-wheeled tenders a rather high and ungainly appearance. Other visual changes have been brought about by the addition of smokebox wing plates to certain engines, whilst others received flared back-plates behind their chimneys. Both devices are typical of Yugoslav practice, the theory being, of course, that they act as miniature smoke deflectors.

Once at work in Yugoslavia, the Liberations became very popular, operating especially on routes radiating from Zagreb and Belgrade. So popular were they in fact that eleven years after the class's arrival in Yugoslavia, a further ten were built at Duro Dakovic locomotive works in Slavonski Brod. Built between 1957 and 1958, these ten engines were almost identical, except for the addition of German-style smoke deflectors and Heinl feed water heaters, both rather altering the engine's appearance. These were almost the last steam engines built for Yugoslavia, the very last being the ubiquitous American 0–6–0T shunters completed by Slavonski Brod in 1959, also originally supplied by U.N.R.R.A. It is significant that Yugoslavia's last steam engines should be to British and American wartime relief designs, so bringing a chequered ending to this country's diverse locomotive traditions. Rather coincidentally, Yugoslavia also received sixty-five American S160s, some through U.N.R.R.A and others from Italy after territorial changes (F.S. 736 class). However these, which the J.Z. classified 37, disappeared during the 1960s.

A few Liberations still survive, principally in the south around Niš, although when I was in Belgrade one was operational on P.W. specials. Never will I forget waiting in the scorching sunlight at Belgrade depot for the Liberation to return from its ballasting trip. It was scheduled back on shed at 13.15, but finally turned up at 17.15. However, my wait was worthwhile, as this was the only Liberation I saw actually in steam. During this time I took opportunity to film the derelict examples on Belgrade's engine dump, the subject of the plate, and apart from this being an important picture historically, it tells the story of British aid engines finally being cast aside by the ever-developing and modernising Yugoslavia, the modern capital city of Belgrade looming up in the background bearing colloquial, though rather romantic, testimony to the fact.

Further value may be attributed to this plate by virtue of its coming from the Serbian republic of Yugoslavia, where railway photography is strictly forbidden. Despite a previous nine months' hard negotiations from Britain, I spent a nerve-racking ten days in Belgrade attempting to gain some authority to film. After much stress, including several arrests, papers were begrudgingly given for photography at Belgrade and Novi Sad – see plate 14 – although it was made clear that the engines were obsolescent, therefore best forgotten, and any publicity I might give to Yugoslavia's use of these and other steam engines was considered of no value whatsoever, if not actually undesirable! It was therefore with some relief, if not guilt, that the plate was made. The Liberations' days are now numbered and with their final passing will disappear another of Britain's distinctive contributions to recent locomotive history. Later on my tour I discovered a line of condemned Liberations, along with some ex-Serbian 01 2–6–2s, outside a remote country scrapyard in Croatia and guessed that these would be some of Croatia's Liberations which latterly worked between Zagreb and Rijeka. It is, however, refreshing to note that both Poland and Czechoslovakia still retain a few active examples.

The S160 2–8–0 will be dealt with in a later volume of this series but some basic comparisons with the Liberations will be of interest:

	Vulcan Liberation 2–8–0	American S160 2–8–0
Cylinders (2)	$21\frac{5}{8}$ in. × 28 in.	19 in. × 26 in.
Driving wheel diameter	4 ft $9\frac{1}{8}$ in.	4 ft 9 in.
Boiler pressure	227 lbs per sq. in.	225 lbs per sq. in.
Grate area	44 sq. ft	41 sq. ft
Axle loading	$18\frac{1}{2}$ tons	15.6 tons
Tractive effort	44,260 lbs	31,490 lbs
Weight in full working order (engine only)	85 tons	72 tons

J.Z. 51 class 2–6–2T   Plate No. 14

A hideous and resounding whistle echoed amid the gloomy depths of Novi Sad depot, and there was a rush of steam only to be followed by a brief silence until, with an almost ethereal motion, this gaunt smoky creature rolled out of the darkness into the afternoon sunshine. Restless and snorting it proceeded, shrouded in smoke, onto the turntable and was soon clanking its way towards the station, impregnating the yards with its odorous presence, whilst its whistle blared like an anguished banshee in the quietness of the afternoon. This rakish piece of Hungarian ironmongery is one of a fleet of such engines still in operation throughout various areas of Yugoslavia. They have been a standard M.A.V. type since early this century, being designed for the light branches and connecting lines which abounded throughout Hungary during the great empire. Designated 375, these 54-ton 2–6–2Ts have an 11-ton axle load, 3 ft 10½-in. driving wheels and a 20-sq.-ft grate area. Simultaneously with their production came the M.A.V.'s similar, but lighter, 376 class 2–6–2s with an axle loading of only 9 tons – later the J.Z. 50 class.

The 375s' introduction in 1907 was rather before superheating became a standard innovation and accordingly they were built as two-cylinder saturated compounds, although piston valves were incorporated. Over the six years between 1907 and 1913 151 locomotives appeared, many with Brotan boilers. However, over these years the M.A.V. became pre-occupied with superheating and decided to superheat four engines from the 1911 batch, two being simples and two compounds, their object being to discover whether any advantage was to be gained by superheating the compounds. The decision went in favour of a superheated engine with simple expansion and so was set a precedent for further building after 1913. No final decision was made regarding Brotan boilers, however, as from the 213 examples built between 1915 and 1923, only seventy-two possessed standard boilers, the remaining 141 being Brotan-fitted. These simple engines underwent some dimensional changes, the original 15½-in diameter (H.P.) and 23¼-in. diameter (L.P.) of the compounds became a standard 16¼-in. whilst the boiler pressure was reduced from 199 lbs per sq. in. to 171 lbs. per sq. in. The 375s may be considered forerunners to the M.A.V.'s 342 2–6–2Ts.

Building then ceased until World War II, when an increase in demand for branch line power led the M.A.V. to produce a further twelve, and after the war another 140 were added, with construction continuing right up to 1959 – over fifty years after the class's inception! A total in excess of 500 was thus built and many of the original saturated compounds were rebuilt to conform, both in Hungary and other lands.

Naturally, not all were destined to remain in Hungary, as the vast reduction of the Empire in 1918 spread them to other lands. Hungary lost Croatia to Yugoslavia and Transylvania to Roumania, many 375s going to the new territories and in Yugoslavia and Roumania the type can still be found today. The S.H.S. received some ninety-eight 375s split roughly as follows: sixty-six saturated compounds and some thirty-two superheated simples, many with Brotan boilers. They became widespread on the lightly-laid routes in Croatia, Vojvodina and central Serbia and in such areas they may still be found eking out their days. All too soon, though, the J.Z. modernisation programme, which so far has put emphasis on the heavier-laid routes, will catch up with them and scenes such as this one will fade into history. Novi Sad depot serves a network of secondary lines throughout the Serbian flatlands.

In 1929, the S.H.S commissioned a further thirty from Maschinen-fabrik, Budapest, whilst between 1941 and 1942 fifteen were actually built in Yugoslavia at Slavonski Brod, this latter batch being identical to the original M.A.V. engines except in their enlarged bunkers, which rather upset the design's symmetry. The end of the war brought a further twenty or so as part of a bulk reparation package, some from Hungary, others coming via Czechoslovakian ownership, in which the Č.S.D. classified them 331.0. Thus Yugoslavia obtained about 160 examples in various ways and although none survives in compound form, some still retain their Brotan boilers.

It is hard to believe that such incredibly antiquated-looking machines could have been constructed less than fifteen years from the present Space Age. Such is man's ever-thrusting progress, today's achievements becoming tomorrow's history with ever-increasing rapidity. I remark upon the kaleidoscopic pattern of design and practice, for who in the world today would have either the desire or the temerity to produce such a doyen of historic engines.

J.Z. 53 class 2–8–2T   Plate No. 56

One of the most interesting aspects of my stay at Maribor was seeing these ex-Austrian Federal Railway (B.B.O.) 2–8–Ts, a small batch of which is allocated there. Two members were stripped down receiving extensive repairs, whilst another was running in after overhaul, resplendent in its freshly-painted black livery. Very few now remain of the twenty-nine which Yugoslavia received as war reparations after 1945. Their duties around Maribor consist of trip and shunting work, especially along the route to the Austrian border at Bleiburg. Their original B.B.O. classification was 378, later becoming 93[13] under the German occupation, and afterwards reverting to the 93 class by which all survivors in Austria are known today. In comparison, the J.Z. engines were classified 53 and numbered 53.001–29.

They are of remarkably modern origin, having been built during the late 'twenties and early 'thirties when the last Austrian steam designs were appearing. The class formed part of a two-engine standardisation plan, using the 378s for secondary lines and the 478 0–8–0 heavy shunting tanks. The standard parts were boilers, motion, axleboxes, wheel centres and water tanks, the 2–8–2s receiving extra wheels in order to restrict their axle load to 11 tons so as to give them freedom over Austria's secondary routes, whilst the 0–8–0, upon which axle loadings were not so important, weighed up to 16 tons. However the 378s' lessened adhesion necessitated a reduction in cylinder volume to $17\frac{3}{4}$ in. $\times$ $22\frac{1}{2}$ in., compared with $20\frac{3}{4}$ in. $\times$ $22\frac{1}{2}$ in. on the 478 class. Both classes were given Schmidt superheaters and in accordance with Austrian practice at that time had Lentz valves actuated by Walschaerts valve gear. Furthermore they were amongst the first classes to receive the more conventional single-door smokebox fronts after Austria's long tradition of double opening ones (see plate 12).

These rugged 2–8–2s proved to be both powerful and efficient, their short-coupled wheelbase of $13\frac{3}{4}$ ft rendering them eminently suitable for difficult secondary routes, whilst in the power range they were capable of lifting 200-ton trains over 1 in 40 gradients. Today they survive as one of the O.B.B.'s most numerous classes, with some forty still operative, the majority being allocated to Mistelbach for operating secondary services north of Vienna. Twenty-five engines of the same design, but with detail variations, were put into service by Czechoslovakia between 1942 and 1944, becoming the C.S.D. 431.0 class.

The engines which passed to the J.Z. have retained their slender Austrian chimneys, whereas most O.B.B. examples were Giesl-fitted some years ago. Nevertheless, one J.Z. engine, No. 53.029, did temporarily receive the injector in 1960, being one of several Yugoslav engines so tested, but the idea was not perpetuated owing to the decision to abandon steam. Although they retain their original chimneys, the plate shows how different they appear thanks to the addition of Yugoslavia's flared chimney back plate. It will be noticed that when the engine is viewed from the rear this creates the illusion of a bulbous-shaped chimney, rather like a wood burner, and as such dramatically alters the engine's appearance.

Most old Austrian types extant in Yugoslavia work in Slovenia and the plate was made at Imeno, a tiny village on the Slovenian – Croatian border, the 53 being seen departing on a nine-mile cross-country run to Stranje. Just prior to the 53's departure an ex-M.A.V. 4-8-0 arrived with a connecting train from Zagreb and the two standing side by side in this remote place were an impressive sight. No preservation plans are as yet made, either in Yugoslavia or Austria, although Austria has earmarked one of the related 0-8-0Ts for the Vienna Railway Museum and possibly this will serve as sufficient representation of both types. The remaining 53 class dimensions are: boiler pressure 199 lbs per sq. in., driving wheel diameter 3 ft 7¼ in. and grate area 22 sq. ft. The engines have a coal and water capacity of 3 tons and 2,200 gallons respectively. See also *Twilight of Steam,* plate 99.

J.Z. 760 mm 83 0-8-2/97 0-6-4 rack and adhesion engines   Plate No. 53

After liberation from the Turks, Bosnia and Hercegovina became a protectorate under the Austrian Empire in 1878. This led to the creation of an extensive 760 mm gauge railway network totalling some 625 miles – as part of the country's development, for over the previous 415 years of Turkish rule the region had remained rather backward. Over their early years these lines sported a diversity of motive power, but some stability was given in 1903 by the introduction from Krauss Linz of these 0-8-2s. Twenty-nine were built between 1903 and 1908, all being two-cylinder saturated compounds, and the Bosnia & Hercegovinan Railways (B.H. St.B.) found them ideal for their heavily graded network, with sufficient adhesion weight for climbing and an ample boiler for rapid production of steam. During this period, however, the B.H.St.B. decided in favour of simples rather than compounds and when further engines were built in 1909, they were superheated simples with piston valves, and consequently differed from the earlier batch in a reduction in boiler pressure from 185 lbs per sq. in. to 171 lbs per sq. in. By 1917, 55 of these simples had been delivered from various builders, so bringing the B.H.St.B. total up to eighty-four engines.

When the Austrian Empire was dissolved in 1918, the Kingdom of Serbs, Croats and Slovenes (S.H.S.) was formed, creating what was later to become Yugoslavia. Further engines were ordered during the 1920s by the S.H.S., with twenty-four from Jung in 1923, followed by forty-four from Budapest between 1923 and 1929. This period between the two wars saw the linking of Bosnia's 760 mm lines with those of adjacent Serbia, which also possessed some 375 route miles to this gauge. Thus Yugoslavia received the longest narrow-gauge main lines in Europe, as Belgrade and Sarajevo, the respective capitals of Serbia and Bosnia, were linked by the 252-mile Cucarika line, which additionally extended westwards from Sarajevo through to Dubrovnik and Titograd – a total run from Belgrade of 517 miles. The addition of many secondary lines resulted in a vast narrow-gauge complex throughout the two republics and these 83s became a most prolific and useful type, although until the S.H.S created a fusion of the systems locomotive policy in Bosnia and Serbia had been separately undertaken. Almost fifty years after the 83s' inception, a further thirty were turned out by the J.Z. from Duro Dakovič Works, Slavonski Brod, in 1948-9, thus bringing the total built to almost 200 engines. Although basically identical, three engines of this last batch were characterised by their dominant combined dome/sand box casings.

Following on from the 83s came the 85 class 2-8-2 introduced in 1930, this design being predominantly an 83 with larger boiler and cylinders plus an additional leading axle. Forty-five 85s were built, the two classes forming a sprightly backbone of motive power over much of the network.

Unfortunately the magnificence of Jugoslavia's 760 mm gauge network is now considerably reduced, many of the longer journeys having recently been altered to standard gauge whilst a new direct standard gauge line is planned between Belgrade and Titograd. Over the surviving 760 mm routes a policy of dieselisation has been adopted and very few steam locomotives now survive.

Two rack sections appeared on the B.H.St.B.'s 760 mm network, one between Konjic and Sarajevo, on the Sarajevo–Dubrovnik line – which, incidentally, was closed and converted to standard gauge during the late 1960s – and the other between Donji Vakuf and Travnik on the Sarajevo–Prijedor line. Although part of this latter run has been altered to standard gauge, the rack section which traverses the Komar Pass is still open and this is the final haunt of these 97 class rack/adhesion 0-6-4s. The B.H.St.B. introduced this class of four-cylinder 0-6-4s in 1894 and thirty-eight were supplied over the following twenty-five years. All came from Floridsdorf Works, Vienna, being constructed to the Abt system, and were a development from a small series of earlier B.H.St.B. rack engines which appeared in 1890.

Principally the design was an 0–6–0 with an articulated four-wheel tender. They had Joy valve gear actuating two cylinders for the adhesion and two for the rack wheels – the class being built to operate over maximum gradients of 1 in 17. A later attempt to build a more powerful rack engine failed and accordingly the 97s were destined to become Yugoslavia's standard 760 mm gauge rack locomotive and in 1972, seventy-eight years after their introduction, the last survivors were still to be found banking trains over the Komar Pass. Their duties nowadays are confined to banking, as diesels operate the main service, with the result that many 97s lie rusting away in the woods at Dolac depot near Travnik. It seems amazing that any should survive at all, as the Travnik–Jajce route, which includes the Komar Pass, is paralleled by one of Yugoslavia's finest roads – an almost certain threat to the line's future. Nevertheless, until they finally disappear, the 97s bring a refreshing ring of vintage to the ever-diminishing 760 mm gauge network of the J.Z. Derelict examples from Konjic also lie at Sarajevo and one of these engines is depicted in the illustration.

Plate 53 epitomises the rundown of this once-magnificent network, showing the breakers yard at Alipaš in Most depot, Sarajevo. In the foreground lies the almost abstract, yet grotesquely representational, mass of a cut-up 97 engine, whilst a condemned 83 looms up forlornly in the background. The interaction of the two masses is made even more poignant by the separating veil of white flowers which add a somewhat funereal innocence to this macabre and grisly scene.

Leading dimensions are:

	J.Z. 83 class 0–8–2		J.Z. 97 class rack/adhesion 0–6–4
Cylinders:			
original compound	$14\frac{1}{2}/21\frac{1}{2}$ in. × $17\frac{3}{4}$ in.	adhesion:	$13\frac{1}{2}$ in. × $17\frac{3}{4}$ in.
standard simple	17 in. × 17 in.	rack:	$14\frac{1}{4}$ in. × $14\frac{1}{4}$ in.
Driving wheel diameter	2 ft $11\frac{1}{2}$ in.	adhesion:	2 ft $7\frac{1}{2}$ in.
		rack:	2 ft 3 in.
Boiler pressure	171 lbs per sq. in.		171 lbs per sq. in.
Grate area	$18\frac{1}{4}$ sq. ft		$17\frac{1}{4}$ sq. ft
Axle load	8 tons		8 tons
Total weight (engine only)	36 tons		25 tons

INDEX